POLISHES
CLEANS

THE MOON IS BLUE

PLAYS BY F. HUGH HERBERT

Kiss and Tell

For Love or Money

For Keeps

Quiet, Please

Hit Me Again

The Moon Is Blue

BY F. HUGH HERBERT

With an Introduction by BEN HECHT

Random House NEW YORK

Published in New York by Random House, Inc., and simultaneously in Toronto, Canada, by Random House of Canada, Limited.

MANUFACTURED IN THE UNITED STATES OF AMERICA

QB

For Barbara

because she never once said "there"

F. H. H.

The Moon Is Blue was first presented by Aldrich & Myers, with Julius Fleischmann, and produced by Otto Preminger, at Henry Miller's Theatre, New York City, on March 8, 1951, with the following cast:

(IN ORDER OF APPEARANCE)

PATTY O'NEILL	Barbara Bel Geddes
DONALD GRESHAM	Barry Nelson
DAVID SLATER	Donald Cook
MICHAEL O'NEILL	Ralph Dunn

Staged by Otto Preminger

Settings and lighting by Stewart Chaney

SCENES

Act One

Scene I. The Observation Tower of the Empire State Building. Early evening.

Scene II. An apartment on East 49th Street. An hour later.

Act Two

The same. Two hours later.

Act Three

Scene I. The same. Several hours later.

Scene II. The Observation Tower of the Empire State Building. The following afternoon.

The entire action of the play takes place in New York City within 24 hours. Spring, 1951.

INTRODUCTION

BY BEN HECHT

Wit is almost as rare in the theatre as it is in politics or the banking business. And it is almost as profitless. In fact, a witty playwright can irritate an audience as quickly as an off-key tenor—as witness the half-century battle between G. Bernard Shaw and the audiences of the world. Mr. Shaw won the battle, but only after time had removed the timeliness of his wit.

The only institution an audience will permit a playwright to lampoon, without rushing him to the pillory, is Sex. But it must be Sex itself and none of its allied institutions such as marriage, infidelity, divorce or, worst of all, disillusion. A playwright tilting a lampoon at these corollaries of Sex will usually find himself in front of a closed theatre with his name vanishing from its façade.

F. Hugh Herbert is one of the few witty writers for the American stage who has managed to land an audience rather than himself in the aisles. The only other names that come to mind are John van Druten, Noel Coward and S. N. Behrman. The two latter practitioners are, however, on the spotty side. They are apt to take a fretful swing at taboo targets—and send all their jests prematurely to the warehouse.

Mr. Herbert's newest play, *The Moon Is Blue,* is the perfect example of successful mental comedy. It is a play whose sole quality is wit. Its plot, characters and problems are almost as naïve as those in a musical show. Its humor, however, is as sharp and literate as the best of Shaw, Coward and Behrman.

The difference, chiefly, between Mr. Herbert and these other rib ticklers is that Mr. Herbert's wit does not seek to adventure against forbidden targets. It confines itself to Sex, minus its aftermaths or affiliated institutions.

The invention of characters who, though obsessed by sex and love, can yet avoid the disturbing overtones of all disillusion is a tour de force of which only Mr. Herbert and Mr. van Druten seem today capable. In *The Moon Is Blue* two men and a girl discuss for an entire evening the problem of whether the heroine will go to bed legally or sinfully without once striking a disagreeable blow at the audience. That is its negative, although important, virtue.

A play, however, cannot succeed by its deft talent for failing to disturb an audience, and Mr. Herbert's comedy has the positive quality of continuous hilarity. It is a hilarity not compounded out of movie or radio jokes or preposterous situations, but out of a literary brilliance. Out of its familiar people and situations emerges something utterly unfamiliar—an evening of fresh and provocative dialogue. It is a dialogue which not only characterizes the three figures in the play but amiably caricatures them. It does not probe their minds on alien and troublesome topics. It exposes only their attitudes on the alluring problem of sex seduction. It does so with taste, insight and drolleries.

And it is a dialogue of more than people. In its bright sentences are the whimsy and confusion of the civilization in which the three characters exist. Mr. Herbert, in fact, is a Crébillon of our cafés and a Molière of our morals. As a Molière he is, as his royalties can testify, a bit on the cautious side. He exposes his characters without malice, pries into their vagaries without ridicule and leaves them for us to laugh at—and admire.

I do not know how *The Moon Is Blue* reads, but I suspect that it reads as gaily as it sounded on the stage where its director, Mr. Otto Preminger, so cleverly placed it, and where critics and audience so eagerly hailed it. It is my experience that when actors seem to bring what the critics call a delightful charm to their roles, it is the playwright who has actually encharmed the actors.

On the stage, *The Moon Is Blue*—devoid of plot and farcical reaches—aroused almost continuous laughter in the audience. That nothing unhappy happened to its characters, that true love triumphed and virginity, a bit endangered, emerged to arrive intact at the altar, is a false gauge with which to measure the virtues of Mr. Herbert's play. I remember, rather, that for the most part it sparkled like fine wine, tasted like it and left nobody drunk or quarrelsome after imbibing it.

ACT ONE

ACT ONE

Scene I

The Observation Tower of the Empire State Building. The stage is empty for a few moments. Then a young girl strolls out. She is about twenty-one. Her name is PATTY O'NEILL. *She wears a light spring coat over a little street dress. She is hatless but wears gloves. She comes downstage, glancing over her shoulder toward the tower as if she were expecting someone. There is a rather amused, excited smile on her face. There is an eager, fresh quality about* PATTY *that is very engaging.*

She stands at the balustrade, gazing out, but out of the corner of her eye she is still watching the tower.

A few moments later a young man enters from the tower. His name is DON GRESHAM. *Over his arm he carries a light, spring overcoat, and he wears no hat. He carries a small package.*

PATTY *is well aware of the fact that he is there, but affects to pay no attention.* DON *comes down to the balustrade. He is whistling with an air of nonchalance. She affects to be absorbed in the slot-machine binoculars nearby.*

DON

(*Finally*)

Why were you in such a tearing hurry?

PATTY

What?

DON

I was just putting away my wallet and I spoke to the woman selling tickets—and, *bingo*—you'd vanished into thin air.

PATTY

I'm sorry. . . . I didn't know for sure whether . . . Why didn't you *say* something?

DON

I *did*. I yelled "Hey!"—but you were already off in a cloud of dust.

PATTY

No, I don't mean then. Why didn't you say something before in the drug store when we—when we first sort of noticed each other? (*Points to his little package*) Why were you buying pumice stone?

DON

Because I get ink on my hands and pumice stone takes it off.

PATTY

Oh. And all those rubber bands—what do you need them for?

DON

(*Amused*)

I need those in my business. I didn't know you were watching me that closely.

PATTY

I was just across the counter from you and I couldn't help hearing, and, besides, I'm always *fascinated* by what other people buy in drug stores. You got razor blades, too.

DON

I shave. You didn't buy anything, I noticed.

PATTY

I was flirting with a divine new shade of lipstick, but it was a dollar-fifty and I decided to be sensible. It's so beautiful too—it's called . . .

(DON *instantly produces a little package from his pocket and puts it on the balustrade in front of her.*)

DON

"Dusty Dawn"—and a damn silly name, if you ask me.

(PATTY *takes a lipstick out of the package and looks at him wonderingly.*)

PATTY

For me?

DON

I rarely use lipstick.

PATTY

How perfectly sweet of you! You must've been watching me in the drug store.

DON

When a man's waiting for pumice stone and rubber bands, he has to watch something.

PATTY

Why didn't you speak to me then?

DON

I was just rehearsing a suitable gambit—when you mooched off.

PATTY

I did not mooch off.

DON

You never looked back once.

PATTY

Well, I should hope not. (*Giggles*) I tried to create the impression that I'd suddenly remembered an urgent appointment.

DON

You almost fooled me. (*They look at each other, smiling*) Why didn't you smile at me like that in the drug store?

PATTY

I don't smile at men in drug stores.

DON

Well, a few minutes later then—when I obviously followed you into the lobby where they sell tickets for up here. It wouldn't have hurt you to smile then.

PATTY

Did I look very aloof?

DON

Aloof and forbidding—and rather scared. You scowled.

PATTY

Nonsense, I was trying to look sultry and provocative.

DON

You beat me to the elevator, too.

PATTY

(*Slightly fussed*)

I know . . . I got in before I realized . . . I wondered what happened to you. (*She yawns vigorously*) Are your ears still popping? Mine are.

DON

That's just your imagination.

PATTY

Don't be silly. Of course they're popping. It's the pressure or something. Haven't you ever been up in an airplane? (*Another yawn*) It's okay now. They un-popped. Now I feel fine. (*Gazes out*) Gosh! Isn't this wonderful?

DON

Not particularly. Fog's coming in. Can't see much today.

PATTY

You can see Staten Island.

DON

(*Amiably*)

You're crazy. You can hardly see a thing.

PATTY

I can.

DON

(*Points*)

You can't even see the Chrysler Building.

PATTY

I can.

DON

You're nuts.

PATTY

Well, I can imagine it, anyway.

DON

Couldn't you imagine it just as well from the street? They told you it was crazy downstairs. Remember the sign: Visibility Poor. Look—There's not a soul up here.

PATTY

I'm glad I came. I love it up here. Just think—we're over a thousand feet up. The tallest building in the world. I think it's wonderful. I mean—just look—doesn't it take your breath away. (*An ecstatic sigh*) It's a wicked extravagance, but I don't care. It's worth every penny of it.

(DON *takes out a dollar bill and two dimes and puts them in front of her on the balustrade.*)

DON

By the way, here's your dollar-twenty.

PATTY

What? What do you mean?

DON

Despite your sultry scowl, I paid for two tickets—and when the woman said you'd paid for yours, I told her we'd had a little spat—so she gave me the money back.

PATTY

You mean you're treating me to this? How perfectly sweet of you. Thanks a lot. (*Puts the money in her purse*) Now I can really enjoy it. One always gets a bigger kick out of things for free. And you don't even know my name, even. I think that's perfectly charming of you. (*Looks him over*) What's your name? Mine's Patty—Patty O'Neill.

DON

Don Gresham.

PATTY

Don. Yes. That suits you. You look like a Don.

DON

Patty, let me ask you a question. I don't usually do things like this, and I have a . . .

(PATTY *pretends to be absorbed in the slot-machine binoculars. She wants to duck questions.*)

PATTY

I wonder how this gadget works?

DON

(*Gives her a dime*)

For a dime you can find out.

PATTY

Thanks. You *are* nice. Before—when you came out, I was pretending.

DON

I gathered that.

(*She drops in the dime and swivels the gadget around. She is enchanted.*)

PATTY

Oh, this is terrific. Now you can really see. . . . Wouldn't you like a look?

DON

I've been up here before. My office is in this building. Patty, listen to me a minute. I'd like to tell you . . .

PATTY

(*Adjusts binoculars*)

Oh, stop jabbering. I want to enjoy this, and I can't while you keep on talking. . . . Are you drumming like that because you're bored or nervous—or do you want to hold my hand? You can if you want to. . . .

(*She takes off her glove and slips her hand into his. He fondles it gently. She gazes into space—with the binoculars and then without. Her face is troubled.*)

DON

You are a screwball—and no fooling. And you have very sweet hands. (*Looks into her face*) What are you thinking about?

PATTY

I want to cry.

DON

What for?

PATTY

(*Points*)

All those people . . .

DON

What people?

PATTY

In Brooklyn.

DON

(*Points over his shoulder*)

Brooklyn's over there.

PATTY

I don't care. It doesn't matter. I still want to cry.

DON

Why?

PATTY

Because it's so sad.

DON

What? Living in Brooklyn?

PATTY

Please don't be funny. I was born in Brooklyn.

DON

I'm not trying to be funny. I swear I don't know what you're talking about.

PATTY

(*In a reverie*)

The poor, drab, little people, sweating their lives out in a . . .

DON

(*Shivering*)

Nobody's sweating on a day like this. Don't worry.

PATTY

Don't be so darn practical.

DON

Then quit talking like a play by Saroyan.

PATTY

I adore him, don't you?

DON

Huh? Who?

PATTY

Saroyan.

DON

I can take him or leave him.

PATTY

I think he's wonderful. (*Into the void*) Hello out there!

DON

Huh?

PATTY

Hello Out There. It's a play of his. Saroyan's. *Hello Out There,* by William Saroyan. It's about a man who was in jail. (*Gently*) He loves little, drab, gentle people. Saroyan—not the man who was in jail.

DON

(*Baffled*)

Look, Patty—let's go down, shall we? It's getting all fogged in.

PATTY

No, I like it up here.

DON

Aren't you cold?

PATTY

Only my hands. They always get cold when I get excited.

DON

What are you excited about?

PATTY

Coming up here. I've wanted to for years.

DON

Then why didn't you?

PATTY

Frankly, because I couldn't afford it. You can get a lovely pair of nylons for a dollar-twenty. I don't know why I decided to splurge tonight.

DON

(*Chuckles gently*)

You're terribly sweet. . . .

PATTY

Look, I swear I had no idea you'd . . . I *was* splurging . . . Fancy charging a dollar-twenty just to ride to the top of a building. It's enough to make you a Communist.

DON

You think Stalin doesn't charge admission to go to the top of the Kremlin?

PATTY

(*Seriously*)

You know, I never thought of that.

DON

Are you hungry?

PATTY

Starving.

DON

Let's go down and get some dinner.

PATTY

(*Shakes her head*)

No.

DON

Why not?

PATTY

You've spent enough on me already.

DON

Don't be silly.

PATTY

You have, too. A ticket to the tower and a lovely lipstick . . .

DON

(*Ribbing*)

Don't forget the dime for the gadget.

PATTY

(*Gravely*)

That's right.

DON

Now, don't be a little dope. We're going someplace to eat. I don't want any arguments out of you.

PATTY

Where would we go?

DON

You name it.

PATTY

Are you very flush?

DON

Just name it.

PATTY

Would you take me to the Stork Club?

DON

Sure.

PATTY

It's awfully expensive.

DON

Oh, well. Mr. Billingsley has to live.

PATTY

Do you like the Stork Club?

DON

I've only been there a few times. It's mostly for people in show business, and I don't know many of those. Do you like it?

PATTY

Gosh, yes. I've only been there once—an agent took me—but I'd just adore to go again. None of the boys I know can afford it. We usually go Dutch to a spaghetti joint. I love spaghetti, don't you?

DON

Frankly, I prefer a good steak. Come on, let's go.

PATTY

(*Hesitates, stalling*)

It's early. I'm not that hungry.

DON

Fine. We'll go to my place first and have a drink. How about it?

PATTY

(*Looks him over for a long time*)

Would you try to seduce me?

DON

(*Amused*)

I don't know. Probably. Why?

PATTY

Why? A girl wants to know.

DON

A girl is supposed to be intuitive about those things. You don't go around bluntly asking people such questions.

PATTY

I do. I always do.

DON

And what happens if they say yes, they're going to try and seduce you?

PATTY

I generally believe them, and then I'm out one dinner.

DON

And if they say their intentions are honorable?

PATTY

I generally believe *them*—but you get fooled sometimes. I hate men like that. After all, there are lots of girls who don't mind being seduced. Why pick on those who do?

DON

Okay. I won't make a single pass at you. Do you believe me?

PATTY

(*A long look*)

Yes. I do. You're nice. I like you.

DON

I could be lying.

PATTY

That's true. Are you?

DON

Frankly, I don't know. I've never run up against anybody like you.

PATTY

(*Delighted*)

How nice!

DON

I won't take an oath that I'm not going to kiss you.

PATTY

Oh, that's all right. Kissing's *fun*. I've *no* objection to that.

DON

I'll be damned if I know whether you're just incredibly naïve or whether you're ribbing the pants off me.

PATTY

(*Bluntly*)

Look, it's very simple. Let's face it—going to a man's apartment almost always ends in one of two ways: Either the girl's willing to lose her virtue—or she fights for it. I don't want to lose mine—and I think it's vulgar to fight for it. So I always put my cards on the table. Don't you think that's sensible?

DON

(*Smiling*)

Okay. Sold. Affection, but no passion. My word of honor.

PATTY

(*Happily*)

"Affection, but no passion." That's *lovely*. You could run for president on that.

(Laughing, he pulls her to him, tilts up her face, and they kiss.)

DON

You're terribly sweet—even if you are a little bit nuts. (*Kisses her. After kiss*) Patty O'Neill. You must be very Irish.

PATTY

Both of my parents were born in Brooklyn, but Pop's Irish from way back. When he gets good and mad, he can even talk with a thick brogue.

DON

What does he do?

PATTY

He's a cop.

DON

Oh. Then you probably have lots of brothers and sisters.

PATTY

No. Why?

DON

I always thought Irish cops had at least ten kids.

PATTY

No. I was the only one. My mother died when I was twelve. She was swell.

DON

You live at home?

PATTY

(*Shakes her head emphatically*)

Uh uh. Irish cops are too strict and old-fashioned, and Pop's a holy terror. All my beaux were scared to death of him. I've been on my own since I was eighteen. (*Looks him over*) Are you married?

DON

No.

PATTY

That's good. You shouldn't get married for ages. You're too young. What do you do?

DON

Architect.

PATTY

Oh, that explains the ink and the pumice stone! Are you a draftsman?

DON

Believe it or not—I'm a full-fledged architect. I can build you anything from a cathedral to a bomb shelter.

PATTY

This'll be a lesson to you. You shouldn't pick up girls in the Empire State Building. Then you get hooked for tickets to the tower, and a dinner at the Stork Club—and no prospects before or after. There's not much percentage in it for you, is there?

DON

It's not every day that I can pick up a charming little lunatic like you.

PATTY

Do you really think I'm nuts?

DON

No, not really. But I'm an architect, and I have a rather orderly mind and lead quite an orderly life.

PATTY

(*Thoughtfully*)

I'm too young to tidy up my life yet. You see, at my age, when you're just learning a lot of new things, you haven't the remotest idea what to keep, or what to discard, or even what to get. You just go on collecting them—and hope for the best.

DON

As for instance?

PATTY

A career, if possible. Failing that—marriage. I'm just dying to get married—but I'm very choosy, so it's not going to be easy. The kind of men I want don't grow on trees.

DON

Do they prowl the lobby of the Empire State Building picking up girls?

PATTY

You didn't pick me up. I made you. My gosh, I did everything but actually drop my handkerchief. (*Amused. Looks in his face, laughing*) But don't worry—you're not the type I'm looking for at all.

DON

No?

PATTY

Nope. You looked sort of forlorn and I wanted to talk to you, but you're much too young. When I get married, I want a nice, middle-aged man with gobs of dough. Preferably one who's been married before and had a simply lousy time. He can have five kids, for all I care.

DON

Doesn't sound very romantic.

PATTY

Oh, pooh! Romance is for bobby-sockers. I'd much rather have a man appreciate me than *drool* over me.

DON

Do you think I have a tendency to drool?

PATTY

(*Thoughtfully*)

Yes, I think you're quite demonstrative. I think that's swell. I'm very affectionate myself.

DON

How old are you?

PATTY

I'll be twenty-one in a few weeks. Old enough to vote. (*Gazes into space—points vaguely*) Just think—every day thousands of people my age become old enough to vote—and none of us really know what to vote for. I always want to cry—the poor, little, ignorant people. . . .

DON

No! No! Don't go Saroyan on me again. I'm getting hungry. Aren't you?

PATTY

Yes—let's go.

DON

And you'll let me take you to my place for a drink first?

PATTY

(*Gravely*)

Yes.

DON

Without any qualms?

PATTY

Without a qualm in the world. (*Hastily*) And I'm not reflecting on your virility either.

DON

Let's leave my virility out of it.

PATTY

Well, I just didn't want to hurt your feelings. (*Philosophically*) Boys are so funny. They're not a bit flattered to be trusted.

DON

You met me ten minutes ago. Why do you trust me so implicitly?

PATTY

(*Simply*)

It sounds awfully corny—but I think you're a man of honor. A girl can tell.

DON

(*Touched*)

You're really terribly sweet.

(*He raises her chin and kisses her gently on the lips.*)

PATTY

Thank you. (*Contented sigh*) I'm so glad you don't mind.

DON

Mind what?

PATTY

(*Brightly—taking his arm*)

Oh, men are usually so bored with virgins. I'm so glad you're not.

(*As they walk toward exit*)

Curtain

ACT ONE

SCENE II

The living room of DON'S *apartment in the East Forties. It is on the fifth floor of a large apartment building, well lit by table and floor lamps. It is a large, very masculine room. Windows look out onto the street. Under these windows there is a narrow window seat of leather. On the left is a door leading to the two bedrooms and on the right is a door to the kitchen. There is a fireplace at right, and, nearby, a comfortable chair with an ottoman. Behind this there is a small, well-stocked portable bar. The lamps are all lit. It's about an hour later. Outside, it's raining, a steady, hissing downpour. The drapes are not yet drawn. There is a backing which shows the dimly lit windows of houses across the street.* PATTY *is curled up comfortably on a large couch. She is studying a blueprint—a building designed by* DON. *She has removed her coat, which hangs over the back of a straight chair. There is a coffee table in front of the couch.* PATTY *has also removed her shoes, which stand neatly under the coffee table, on which she has placed her purse and gloves.* PATTY'S *feet are curled up under her, modestly covered by her skirt. Behind the couch, there is a library table with a handsome, massive table lamp. On the table, there is a large silver-framed photograph of a pretty girl. It is a studio portrait of the glamor type. There is no sign of* DON. *After a few moments, the phone rings. The telephone, on a long cord, is on the library table behind the couch.*

PATTY

(Yelling toward kitchen)

Hey! Telephone! (*Silence*) Do you want me to answer it?

(DON *enters from kitchen. He is preparing to fix drinks and carries an ice-bucket in one hand. He sets the ice-bucket down on the bar and then crosses to answer the phone.*)

DON

No, I'll get it. (*Into phone*) Hello? (*Very cordial*) Oh, hello, Mike—sorry, pal, not tonight. Just going out. Sure, later this week. Love to. So long.

(*He hangs up and crosses to bar, where he mixes drinks.*)

PATTY

Who's Mike?

DON

Friend of mine.

PATTY

Are you mad at him?

DON

No, of course not. Why?

PATTY

Why did you hang up so quickly?

DON

(Amused)

Because there wasn't anything more to say. He wanted me to dine with him, and I told him I couldn't.

PATTY

Yes—but you could have talked to him. I always talk by the hour to my friends.

DON

I'll bet you do. (*Glancing around*) Where did I put that bottle of Vermouth?

PATTY

(*Pointing*)

Over there. (*Unrolling blueprint further*) This is fascinating. What's it going to be? Oh . . . I see. . . . (*Reads from blueprint*) Ground plan—Freeport Civic Center—Donald Gresham, architect. . . . Oh, boy, that's something. Are you famous?

DON

No. Not in the least. I'm just a good, practical, modern, run-of-the-mill architect. (*Hands her another rolled-up blueprint*) You can get a better idea from this. It's an elevation.

(*She removes rubber band from rolled-up plan, spreads it out. He mixes cocktail thoughtfully.*)

PATTY

Now I know why you needed rubber bands. (*Looks at plan*) That's swell. Is it built already?

DON

Building now.

PATTY

Have you planned many buildings?

DON

Quite a few. Used to be with a big firm. Went on my own a couple of years ago.

PATTY

Don't you get an awful kick out of looking at a building—and knowing that it all started in your head?

DON

Sure. I'll let you in on a secret. First job I did off my own

bat was a large, hideous warehouse. I sometimes drove out late at night when there wasn't a soul around and I sat in my car and gloated over it.

PATTY

All alone?

DON

Uh huh. Large, boxlike brick warehouses don't appeal to many people.

PATTY

I think it's more fun to have someone to gloat *with.*

DON

Might be. Are you sure you won't have a martini?

PATTY

Quite sure. I only want a lemonade, that's all. Or a Coke, or something.

DON

I'm sorry, but I'm fresh out of lemons and/or Cokes.

PATTY

Never mind. I'll settle for an olive. I really don't want a thing.

DON

Don't you like martinis?

PATTY

I used to like them, but I gave up drinking.

DON

Why?

PATTY

I think it's sort of high school to drink and smoke when you don't actually crave it. (*Looking around*) I love your apartment. Do you live here alone?

DON

(*Fixing martinis*)

All alone.

PATTY

But you showed me two bedrooms.

DON

One's for guests—if, as and when I have guests.

PATTY

Oh. (*Slight pause*) Do you have a mistress?

DON

Mistress? Isn't that a rather old-fashioned term?

PATTY

Well, it may be old-fashioned but at least it's specific. Do you have one?

DON

You ask the damnedest questions.

PATTY

Why? You're a bachelor, and you're obviously quite well off. It's a natural question.

DON

It isn't a bit natural. You don't go around asking people bluntly if they have a mistress.

PATTY

I do. It saves so much time. I mean, one always finds out sooner or later. Do you? Have one, I mean?

DON

No, as a matter of fact, I don't.

PATTY

That's good. I'm glad. (*A pause*) Why *don't* you have one? (*Hastily*) You needn't tell me unless you want to.

DON

Well, maybe I think it's sort of high school to have a mistress unless you actually crave one.

PATTY

(*Promptly*)

You know, that's really very true. (*Points to picture*) Who's that?

DON

Her name is Cynthia.

PATTY

She's quite cute. (*A closer look*) Very cute. (*A questioning look*) Are you in love with her?

DON

(*Vaguely*)

No. Not now. I used to be. Sort of, I think. I don't know. Not any more, anyway.

PATTY

Oh. Why do you have her picture?

DON

Because she gave it to me.

PATTY

Is she in love with you?

DON

How can a man tell?

PATTY

When a girl gives a man her picture, that's usually a sign.

DON

I dunno. Could be. Probably thought she was. She's only eighteen.

PATTY

Were you engaged?

DON

(*Gloomily*)

More or less, I suppose.

PATTY

(*Compassionately*)

Oh. How sad for you! (*Looks at picture again*) She's so pretty. Was she . . . ?

DON

(*Grimly*)

She was *not* my mistress.

PATTY

I never said she was.

DON

You were just going to!

PATTY

Don't be disagreeable. (*Brightly*) You're not engaged to her now? I mean, not even *sort* of?

DON

Nope. All off.

PATTY

When did you split up?

DON

Last night. Or maybe this morning. Sometime in between.

PATTY

Oh. How sad! Were you crushed? I'm always simply devastated when I break up with people. I was engaged to a boy once, and when I sent him back the ring, I absolutely wept buckets.

DON

Never gave Cynthia a ring, and the only time she ever weeps is into the fifth daiquiri.

PATTY

What an *awful* thing to say. I don't believe you even liked her.

DON

I'm beginning to wonder about that myself.

PATTY

Then why are you so unhappy about it?

DON

I'm not a bit unhappy.

PATTY

You're keeping her picture. And when I asked if you were still in love with her, you shilly-shallied.

DON

(*Cheerfully*)

Okay, she's left an aching void in my heart.

PATTY

Is that why you picked me up—sort of on the rebound?

DON

Could be.

PATTY

Why did you split up?

DON

You ask too many questions.

PATTY

I know. I'm sorry. (*Looks at picture again*) She has a very pretty chin.

DON

She's very pretty all over.

PATTY

(*Significantly*)

Oh. How sad! Then she *was* your mistress?

DON

She was nothing of the sort.

PATTY

You said she was pretty all over. I naturally thought . . .

DON

Why are you so preoccupied with sex?

PATTY

(*Indignant*)

Who? Me?

DON

Yes—you.

PATTY

Do you really think I am?

DON

Well, you're always asking people if they plan seduction, or whether they're bored with virgins, or if they have a mistress. If that isn't being preoccupied with sex, I'd like to know what is.

PATTY

You may be right. (*Brightly*) But don't you think it's better for a girl to be preoccupied with sex than occupied?

DON

(*Strolls to window*)

You win. Much better. (*Peers through drapes*) Raining like hell.

PATTY

(*Rises, points to the TV set*)

Say, listen, is your TV working?

DON

Sure, why?

PATTY

What's the time?

DON

About seven-twenty.

PATTY

Oh, well, there's lots of time yet. Can you watch TV from the Stork Club?

DON

I don't know.

PATTY

Remind me to turn it on at ten, will you? They're doing a show on CBS that I'd have been absolutely perfect for, but they gave it to another girl and I want to see if she stinks. It was a nice little part too.

DON

What kind of parts do you play?

PATTY

Well, I've only done three dramatic shows so far—the competition is simply brutal—but each time I've done a sort of—

well, I suppose you'd call it a sort of tart. I'm good, too. I got a call from Studio One. Friday I'm going to read for another tart.

DON

You don't look very much like a tart.

PATTY

I do on TV. I look all haggard and dissipated and simply crawling with vice.

DON

Doesn't that apply to everyone on TV?

PATTY

Don't you be snotty about TV. Maybe some of the shows are rather crummy yet, but it's bread and butter to hundreds of girls like me.

DON

Talking of bread and butter—I'm hungry. Let's go and eat.

PATTY

Okay.

DON

You're going to get drenched without a raincoat.

PATTY

Let's not go out! Let's fix dinner up here. I'm a sensational cook.

DON

Unfortunately, I haven't any sensational food.

PATTY

Don't you have anything?

DON

Afraid not.

PATTY

No leftovers? What I can do with leftovers is nobody's business. Do you like kedgeree?

DON

Beg pardon?

PATTY

Kedgeree—it's made with finnan haddie. Do you have any finnan haddie?

DON

God, no.

PATTY

Don't say "God, no" like that. You've never tasted it. It's delicious.

DON

Look, Patty—all I have in the kitchen is a box of crackers that are very stale, and a small crock of cheese that was sent to me last Christmas.

PATTY

Blue cheese?

DON

It's going blue. That's all. No eggs even, no milk—nothing.

PATTY

Don't you ever eat meals here?

DON

No.

PATTY

No wonder you're unhappy and maladjusted.

DON

I'm not a bit unhappy, and my adjustment is just dandy.

PATTY

You broke up with Cynthia.

DON

It was not for lack of home cooking, believe me.

PATTY

How do you know? I think that's awful. That darling kitchen going to waste. And that lovely ice box and stove. I want to cry. Honestly.

DON

You're the strangest girl I've ever known.

PATTY

You don't know me. You picked me up.

DON

You don't have to rub it in.

PATTY

Yes, I do. I think both of us ought to bear it in mind all the time.

DON

Why?

PATTY

Because— (*A sigh*) I just think we should, that's all.

DON

Why?

PATTY

Just in case we start feeling romantic about each other.

DON

Is that bad?

PATTY

Yes. You picked me up, and no matter what happened, you'd always wonder.

DON

What about?

PATTY

About all the other men who might have picked me up before you did—in just the same way.

DON

I have been wondering about that. Do you do it often?

PATTY

Once is enough to leave doubts.

DON

Mine are completely dispelled.

PATTY

For the time being. They'd come creeping back, though.

DON

(*Earnestly*)

Never. You see, you're rather . . .

PATTY

Oh, shut up. I don't want to talk about it any more.

DON

Okay. Would you like to fix dinner for us here?

PATTY

Even I can't do much with stale crackers and moldy old cheese.

DON

There's a market down the block. I have a raincoat. I could get whatever you need.

PATTY

(*She's obviously enchanted*)

Would you like to?

DON

Sure. Would you?

PATTY

I'd love it. I adore cooking, and I rarely get a chance to cook for a man. My roommate's a girl.

DON

(*Amused*)

I'm relieved to hear it.

PATTY

(*Smiling at him*)

Now who's preoccupied with sex?

DON

Okay, okay. What'll I buy?

PATTY

Let's splurge. Let's have steak and mushrooms and a salad and cake and coffee. And strawberries. You'll have to buy a sponge cake. I won't have time to bake one. Be sure to get whipping cream, and we'll have a strawberry shortcake.

DON

Okay. Sold. Make out a list.

PATTY

Oh, you don't need a list. Tell them at the store that you haven't anything—tell 'em what we're going to have and they'll tell you what you need. Tell 'em you're just setting up housekeeping.

DON

All right. (*The phone rings. She glances at it then at him. He picks up receiver*) Hello? Oh, hello, Shirley. How are you, baby? No, not tonight, I'm afraid. Nope—dining with an important client. Give me a raincheck, will you? Okay, Shirley. Be seeing you. 'Bye.

(*He hangs up.*)

PATTY

Who's Shirley?

DON

Girl I know. Blonde, blue eyes. Hundred and ten pounds. Very beautiful. All over. Any more questions?

PATTY

What did she want?

DON

She asked me to dinner. She lives with her parents. They're out tonight.

PATTY

Oh. Personally, I don't think it's right for girls to call men up.

DON

(*Ribbing*)

It *is* rather disgusting, isn't it?

PATTY

I know what you're thinking. I picked you up—and that's worse than calling up.

DON

Will you stop harping on that—you sweet little dope?

(*He moves toward her. She backs away. He takes her by the shoulders.*)

PATTY

Run along and do your marketing.

DON

(*Gently*)

Patty—I . . .

PATTY

(*Deliberately matter-of-fact*)

And don't forget the staples—the flour, and salt and sugar and coffee and stuff . . . (*She wriggles herself free of his hands on her shoulders. He stands looking at her very intently*) Well, go on—what are you waiting for?

DON

I've decided not to run for president—at least not on that platform you drafted for me.

PATTY

What?

DON

"Affection but no passion." I think . . .

PATTY

You're not passionate now—you're just hungry. And so am I. Go out and get the groceries.

DON

Okay. (*Gets his raincoat*) I'll be back in a flash. Hold the fort.

PATTY

Hey, wait! What'll I do if the phone rings while you're gone?

DON

Answer it.

PATTY

Aren't you afraid of being compromised?

DON

Not particularly. Of course, if my mother called at four A.M. and a girl answered, she might raise an eyebrow, but it's only seven P.M. and my mother's in Europe.

(PATTY *has walked to the door with him. Suddenly she points to a framed picture.*)

PATTY

Did you build this house?

DON

Not yet. Some day I plan to. It's just a sketch. It's a sort of hideaway cabin.

PATTY

I like it. Of course you'll never find lovely old trees like that.

DON

(*Takes picture off hook*)

The trees are already there. I plan to build this shack to fit into the trees.

PATTY

How do you mean?

DON

It's a piece of property I own.

PATTY

Gosh? Do you own property?

DON

Don't be too impressed. It's just five acres of land up in Maine. Cost me all of a thousand dollars. (*He laughs*) Bought it four years ago—and went in hock to pay for it. Clear now.

PATTY

Oh. Is that where you'd have lived if you'd married Cynthia?

DON

She didn't like it.

PATTY

You're kidding. She didn't like this darling cabin?

DON

She said she didn't want to live in a neck of the woods up in Maine.

PATTY

Why not? She's crazy.

DON

No, she isn't. You'd be surprised at the number of people who don't want to live in Maine.

(PATTY *stands gazing at picture. He looks over her shoulder.*)

PATTY

What's this long, flat business?

DON

Influence of Frank Lloyd Wright. Car port under it—sun deck on top. Modern as hell.

PATTY

Is this the bedroom?

DON

Yep. Windows on three sides. Fireplace here. Huge fireplace. Roast an ox on it, if you felt like it.

PATTY

It might be fun to roast an ox in a bedroom.

DON

Limb of that oak tree just misses the sun deck by two feet. That's quite a tree.

PATTY

(*She stares at him*)

It must be wonderful to own a tree.

DON

Huh?

PATTY

I have a window box with geraniums—but it must be simply terrific to actually own an enormous tree.

DON

(*Indulgently*)

I own a stream, too. (*Points to picture*) It's way back there. It's barely a trickle, but it does flow. It could be dammed up to make a swimming hole.

PATTY

How wonderful! Do you ever drive out to gloat over it?

DON

My child, it's a good sixteen-hour drive. Haven't seen it for a couple of years. Only remember that I own it when I pay the taxes.

PATTY

If I owned an oak tree, I'd live in it.

DON

Want to drive out with me some week end and look at it?

PATTY

(*after a long pause*)

No.

DON

Why not?

PATTY

(*Unhappily*)

Because I hinted—and I didn't mean to.

DON

I'd have asked you even if you hadn't hinted. I have rather an affinity for trees myself.

PATTY

When I was a kid . . . (*Stops short—a new thought*) Do you like children?

DON

(*Poker-faced*)

Can't stand the sight of them.

PATTY

Why not?

DON

(*Amused*)

Oh. They're all right, I guess. I've never been exposed to them very much.

PATTY

Isn't that funny? You're quite proud of loving trees, but you're a little ashamed to admit you like kids. I'd like to have at least five.

DON

I know. You plan to acquire them ready-made with a rich middle-aged husband.

PATTY

Oh, yes, but I'd like five of my own too. I suppose you think it isn't fair to bring kids into this—this mess of a world?

DON

Ever hear of a mess being cleaned up by unborn kids?

PATTY

(*Soberly*)

I never thought of it that way.

DON

Think about it while I get all this food you've ordered.

PATTY

Okay. I will. (*Pause*) How old are you?

DON

Twenty-eight. Why?

PATTY

Twenty-eight. Let's see—half that is fourteen—plus seven . . . (*Smiles happily*) Twenty-one. Isn't that amazing? It just works out.

DON

What does?

PATTY

Haven't you ever heard that the girl is supposed to be half the man's age, plus seven?

DON

What girl? What man?

PATTY

Never mind. Beat it.

DON

(*Walks to door, pensively*)

Say, I think I'll get some ham and eggs, too.

(*After his exit* PATTY *goes to table and gets plate of olives, carries it to couch, settles herself comfortably with phone from sofa table and dials.*)

PATTY

(*Into phone*)

Hello, Vicki? Hello, sweetie. Were you getting worried about me? Well, don't. I'm okay, but I won't be home for dinner. No, you can eat up all the spaghetti, you lucky girl. (*Munches on olives*) What? I am not chewing gum. I'm eating olives—and you'll never guess where. I'm in a man's apartment. Now, please stop worrying. No, you don't know him, but he's just divine. What? No, he wouldn't harm a fly, honestly. His name's Gresham—Donald Gresham—and he's an architect and he has a perfectly darling apartment on East 49th Street—and he's a bachelor—and he has a crew haircut—and he owns a perfectly gorgeous old oak tree—oak tree, that's right. . . . Never mind, I'll explain it later. What? I don't know, sweetie—I only met the man a couple of hours ago—No, no, don't worry. . . . He's practically a child, and very sweet. . . . Don't worry. Does he know what? (*She laughs*) Sure. Sure. I told him—and he doesn't mind a bit. Isn't that refreshing? Okay then, stop worrying. Any messages? Oh, how very dull. (*Door buzzer sounds*) Look, I'll call you back later, maybe. There's someone at the door. G'bye.

(*She hangs up, primps and goes to the front door. Enter* DAVID SLATER. DAVID *is around forty and is endowed with entirely too much charm for his own good. Despite the fact that he's tanned and healthy, there's a vague aura of dissipation about him. He speaks with a marked Southern drawl.* DAVID *also has too much money for his own good. It is doubtful if he ever did a day's work in his life. He wears obviously expensive but very informal-looking clothes. At the moment, he has on a raincoat (dry) over a rather hearty tweed suit. He wears a brown felt hat at a rather rakish angle. When* PATTY *opens the door to him, he is obviously very much surprised. He remains in the doorway, gaping at her.*)

DAVID

Well, I'll be damned!

PATTY

(*Smiling*)

Why will you be damned?

DAVID

I'm sorry. You caught me off base. I didn't expect to find—a girl here.

PATTY

Why not? It's a very respectable hour.

DAVID

(*Fussed*)

Yes—yes, of course. I didn't mean—you see, is—er—is Mr. Gresham in?

PATTY

No, but he'll be back in a little while. He went to the market at the corner. Won't you come in?

DAVID

(*Hesitating*)

Well, I was just going out—and I thought maybe Don was free—and—you see, I live a couple of floors above—so I guess I'd better just . . .

PATTY

Don't be silly. Come in. Would you like a drink?

DAVID

(*Gravely*)

I would like a drink very much indeed. (*Disarmingly*) Frankly, I'm still slightly hung over from—er—from last night, and a drink . . .

PATTY

(Soothingly)

I know. A hair of the dog. You'll be all right. I've cured more hangovers than you could shake a stick at.

DAVID

(Shuddering)

Never shake a stick at a hangover. It brings on the screaming willies.

(DAVID *comes in, removes his hat and coat, throws them on window seat, while* PATTY *pours him a drink.*)

My name's David Slater. What's yours?

PATTY

Patty. Patty O'Neill.

DAVID

Known Don for long?

PATTY

(Glibly)

Oh, yes. Of course, it isn't really long—but it just seems like ages. He's a darling. I'm crazy about him.

(Brings him his drink.)

DAVID

(Sipping his cocktail)

That's very interesting. Is he crazy about you?

PATTY

Oh, it's purely platonic on both sides.

(DAVID *glances significantly at her stockinged feet.*)

DAVID

(Very skeptical)

Of course.

PATTY

(*Amused*)

I took off my shoes because my feet hurt.

DAVID

You should never say that your feet hurt.

PATTY

Why not? They do.

DAVID

My foot singular hurts is an intriguing statement. My feet plural hurt is a rather sordid admission.

PATTY

(*Laughs, puts on her shoes*)

Well, anyway, these were on sale at less than half price, and they're divine, but they're too tight. They were killing me. (*She sees that he's finished his cocktail and pours him another*) Here, there's lots left.

DAVID

Aren't you having one?

PATTY

No, thanks. I don't drink. Have you known Don long?

DAVID

Oh, about a year. Little less. Since he moved in here.

PATTY

(*Points to picture*)

Do you know Cynthia?

DAVID

Yes, indeed.

PATTY

She was sort of Don's fiancée, you know. I mean—so to speak.

DAVID

What do you mean—so to speak?

PATTY

Well, it seems to have been a sort of loose arrangement.

DAVID

Loose? Did he say it was loose?

PATTY

Oh, no. But anyway it's all off now.

DAVID

Yes. I know.

PATTY

Was she a pill?

DAVID

That's a rather difficult question.

PATTY

Why? Either she was or she wasn't.

DAVID

It's not quite as simple as that.

PATTY

Why isn't it?

DAVID

Well, since you must know, Cynthia happens to be my daughter.

PATTY

Oh. Oh, I see. I see what you mean.

DAVID

That's good.

PATTY

I'm terribly sorry. If I'd had any *idea* you were her father, I wouldn't have dreamed of asking you if she was a pill.

DAVID

(*Sadly*)

You couldn't have come to a better source. She is.

PATTY

(*Mulling this over*)

Uh huh. I see. . . . (*Handsomely*) Well, anyway, she's awfully pretty. (*Brightly*) Don went out to buy steaks. I'm going to fix dinner up here. I'm a terrific cook. Do you like steak?

DAVID

Mad about it.

PATTY

Why don't you stay and have dinner with us?

DAVID

I think not, thanks very much all the same.

PATTY

Oh, you mean because of Cynthia?

DAVID

There's a connection.

PATTY

Did they split up because of you? I mean, did you disapprove or something?

DAVID

On the contrary. I was prepared to love him like a son. More than a son. I've been practically fawning on him—ready to give my blessing any moment. Damn.

PATTY

Oh. Is Cynthia all broken up about it?

DAVID

No. She doesn't break up so easily. But I am. I was counting on that boy. (*Sighs*) Damnation.

PATTY

Then you're sore because they split up. (*Disarmingly*) You see, I don't know anything about what happened except that he told me it was off.

DAVID

(*Growling*)

Uh huh.

PATTY

You seem to be sore at Don. Are you? I mean, did he do something he shouldn't have done?

DAVID

That's what I'd like to find out. That's why I'm here. (*Grimly*) The theory prevails that Mr. Donald Gresham should be horsewhipped. By me.

PATTY

Why?

DAVID

That's what Cynthia said this morning. (*A pause*) I think.

PATTY

Don't you know?

DAVID

I was not in good shape this morning. She said a lot of things.

PATTY

Like what?

DAVID

Well, it appears that he—I think the phrase is "played fast and loose" with my daughter's affections.

PATTY

That doesn't sound like Don.

DAVID

It isn't Don whom I'm quoting.

PATTY

Oh. Mrs. Slater?

DAVID

Nope. She divorced me years ago. "Fast and loose" was Cynthia's rather dull cliché. (*Sadly*) There's that word "loose" again. Unfortunate.

PATTY

Did she send you down just now to horsewhip poor Don?

DAVID

No. She's out somewhere. She's always out. I never know where she is. (*Sighs*) I was not cut out to raise a daughter.

PATTY

She needs a good influence. She probably needs a mother.

DAVID

Either that—or a good swift kick in the pants.

PATTY

Well, couldn't you provide one or the other? You look awfully young. Why don't you marry again?

DAVID

Unfortunately, all the women to whom I am attracted are not a desirable influence.

PATTY

Then why don't you kick her in the pants?

DAVID

It's an attractive thought. (*Starts to rise*) Well, I've enjoyed our chat, I think I'll . . .

PATTY

Don't dash off. You don't want to eat alone. Stay here. Don't be silly. Come on, do stay.

DAVID

No. I don't think so. I . . .

PATTY

Look, just because they seem to have had a fight is no reason why you . . . (*She breaks off—muses*) Why did they break it off, anyway?

(DAVID *considers for a moment, frowning. He can't quite make this girl out. He settles down again.*)

DAVID

Look, since you seem to know him pretty well, tell me something. Do you consider our friend a man of high principles?

PATTY

I certainly do. He's charming.

DAVID

(*Ruefully*)

I have been told that I am not without charm, but I have no principles whatsoever. Answer my question: is he a man who . . . ?

PATTY

I don't know what you're driving at.

DAVID

(*Unhappily*)

You would if you were a father.

PATTY

Oh. Are you worried about Cynthia?

DAVID

Extremely worried.

PATTY

Is she pregnant?

DAVID

(*Startled*)

Good God, no! (*Suddenly*) What made you ask that question?

PATTY

Well, isn't that what fathers are usually so worried about?

DAVID

I guess it is.

PATTY

My father used to worry himself sick about it. If a boy so much as looked at me, he'd go on and on about hell fire and damnation.

DAVID

Do you believe in that?

PATTY

(*Dubiously*)

No. But it makes you stop and think.

DAVID

I must make a note of that: speak to Cynthia about hell fire and damnation.

PATTY

Yes, but don't go on and on. That's one reason I left home. Pop never drew the line. When boys took me out on a first date they used to get a load of brimstone right off the bat. It scared them all off.

DAVID

I wonder if Cynthia . . .

PATTY

(*Cheerfully*)

Look, you needn't worry. I don't know anything about Cynthia, but Don would never do a thing like that. He doesn't believe in it. Just forget it. (*Brightly*) Is that why you came down? Because you thought she was pregnant?

DAVID

No! I suspected that maybe they . . . (*Suddenly*) Let's talk about something else, shall we?

PATTY

Then you will stay for dinner, won't you?

DAVID

Frankly, I'm tempted. But hadn't we better check with Don first?

PATTY

Why? I'm sure it'll be okay with him. You said you always got along fine. Cynthia doesn't have to know.

DAVID

I wasn't thinking of Cynthia at the moment.

PATTY

What were you thinking about?

DAVID

Well, if I had inveigled a pretty girl to fix dinner for me in my apartment on a rainy night, and somebody tried to crash the party, I'd be sore as hell.

PATTY

Did you say "invaygled"?

DAVID

(*Hastily apologetic*)

Yes, but I assure you I . . .

PATTY

Is that how it's pronounced? I always say "inveigled." Is "invaygled" right?

DAVID

I think so. (*Tries them both*) Inveigled—invaygled—inveigled. Now I don't know. Silly word, isn't it?

PATTY

Well, whichever it is, Don didn't have much to do of it. It was my idea. You see, I didn't bring a raincoat, and he wanted to take me out, and then it started pouring—so I said I'd fix steaks. I make a divine steak sauce. Oh, gosh, I hope he brings mustard.

DAVID

Nevertheless, the fact remains . . .

PATTY

What fact?

DAVID

You and he will doubtless wish to be alone.

PATTY

Why?

DAVID

He may have plans for after dinner.

PATTY

(*Cheerfully*)

Oh, no, that's all understood. He promised he wouldn't even try to make passes. Not one pass, he said, and not one pass has he made. This is purely a social visit—by mutual agreement.

DAVID

Has it occurred to you that after a steak dinner he might become more affectionate?

PATTY

Oh, I hope he will. I like being kissed. (*Musing*) D'you know that he's never even kissed me since the Empire State Building.

DAVID

You mean since it was built?

PATTY

Don't be silly. That's where we met—in a lovely fog. (*Musing*) Gosh, I hope he brings pepper and salt and stuff. Men always like their food well seasoned, but they never *think* of buying it. Do you like kedgeree?

DAVID

Never met her.

PATTY

Kedgeree's a dish.

DAVID

I'll bet she is.

PATTY

It's a dish made of flaked finnan haddie and rice and eggs.

DAVID

I've lost all interest.

(*Telephone rings.*)

PATTY

Excuse me. (*Picks up phone*) Hello—yes—just a sec—I'll look—yes, this is Plaza 9-8416—no—I'm afraid he's not here right now. But he'll be back in a few minutes. What? Oh, not more than another ten minutes, I'd say. He just went out to buy some steaks and groceries—that can't take him so very long. Oh, yes, I'm sure he'll be here—I'm fixing dinner for us and it's such lousy weather that I'm sure we'll stay home afterwards. Shall I tell him who called? Hello? Hello? H'um—hung up on me. (*Hangs up—dubiously*) I can't help it. He told me to answer the phone.

DAVID

Male or female?

PATTY

Female. Very female. She has such a pretty voice. A thick Southern accent that you could cut with a knife.

DAVID

(*Gulping*)

Oh—oh.

PATTY

You know her?

DAVID

Yes, indeed. That must've been Cynthia.

PATTY

Of course—you have a Southern accent, too. I might've guessed. I'm sorry. If I'd had any idea I'd have told her you were here and you could've . . .

DAVID

Thank God you didn't.

PATTY

Why? Didn't you tell me she asked you to come down and horsewhip poor Don?

DAVID

(*Significantly*)

Yes, but—well, never mind. You see—we—never mind.

PATTY

(*Amiably*)

Okay. It's none of my business, anyway. (*Hospitably*) Go on, fix yourself another drink.

DAVID

(*Crosses to bar*)

Don't mind if I do.

PATTY

Would you like me to turn on the TV?

DAVID

Is it in color?

PATTY

You're crazy. It won't be in color for years.

DAVID

Let's wait till then!

(PATTY *goes over to the windows, pulls aside the drapes, presses her nose to the pane, looking out.*)

PATTY

Gosh, it's raining cats and dogs. (*Suddenly*) What kind of a car do you drive?

DAVID

Lincoln. Why?

PATTY

Have you seen the new Cadillac?

DAVID

Yes.

PATTY

They have a fascinating new gadget. Whenever it starts to rain, you press a little button and it squirts water onto your windshield so that the wiper won't get it all smeared. I think of it the moment it starts to rain.

DAVID

(*Sizing her up*)

You drive a Cadillac?

PATTY

Heavens, no! Don't be silly. But the boy Vicki goes with has one, and he lets me work it. Not drive it. Work the gadget. Vicki says . . .

DAVID

Who's Vicki?

PATTY

My roommate. You'd like her. She's wonderful. She's only a year older than I am, but she clucks over me like an old hen. She's a Conover model. This boy with the Cadillac is mad about her, and it's so sad, because he's married and has two kids and he won't do anything to distress his wife. He's a Princeton man.

DAVID

Is that what you are—a model?

PATTY

(*Modestly*)

Well, yes—sort of. I've modeled bras and girdles. Lots of girls don't like to. I don't either, for that matter. But I'm built right for it, and it pays awfully well. And a girl has to eat.

DAVID

What else do you do?

PATTY

Oh, any old thing that comes along. Salesgirl, receptionist, temporary jobs. Just to keep the pot boiling.

DAVID

What's it boiling for? What do you want to do?

PATTY

Act. I'm an actress. Or rather, I want to be an actress.

DAVID

(*This seems to explain everything*)

Oh.

PATTY

I know. The woods are full of 'em. Dime a dozen. I know.

DAVID

Are you any good?

PATTY

I think I'm pretty good!

DAVID

Have you been in many plays?

PATTY

I've been in three TV shows.

DAVID

Oh, does that count?

PATTY

Don't you ever watch TV?

DAVID

They have it in one of my favorite saloons, but I can't say I actually watch it. Last night they had a Roller Derby. God, those poor girls! (*Slight pause*) Don't you find it awfully exhausting?

PATTY

I don't roller skate. I act.

DAVID

I know, I know.

PATTY

(*Pensively*)

Does Cynthia do anything—I mean like acting or modeling or something?

DAVID

No.

PATTY

Doesn't she do anything?

DAVID

No. At least nothing that fills me with paternal pride.

PATTY

Oh. (*Pause*) Do you do anything to make her proud of you? (*He chews on this a second, rises, puts drink down, crosses to sofa and lies down.* PATTY *rises*) What's the matter?

DAVID

You just connected with a vicious left hook below the belt.

(PATTY *sits down on the couch next to him.*)

PATTY

I meant to. I always get burned up with parents who gripe about their kids. It's the parents' fault—that's what I always say.

DAVID

Don't say it again.

PATTY

Why?

DAVID

Because it's a dull thing to say—trite, banal and painfully true.

PATTY

It's never too late to mend.

DAVID

I'll bet you always say that, too.

PATTY

Well, it's true. You've probably got the makings of a very good father. (*She leans close, looking him over*) I like the way your eyes sort of crinkle. You're really very cute. (*He gets up suddenly and walks over to the window. She remains on the couch, looking at him*) Why did you get up?

DAVID

It seemed like a good idea.

PATTY

Why? We were just . . .

DAVID

Frankly, my child, I felt a sudden, powerful, very ignoble desire to kiss the hell out of you.

PATTY

(*Pleased*)

You did? How lovely! This *is* one of my good days. (*This is said rather smugly.*)

DAVID

And, rather than yield to this ignoble desire . . .

PATTY

What's so ignoble about it? I think it's wonderful to be desired. As a rule, I don't attract men, physically, I mean. Not right off the bat, anyway. Vicki says I scare 'em off because I look too wholesome. Who wants to look wholesome? Gosh, I'd love to be so pretty that I could drive men absolutely crazy.

DAVID

You attract me.

PATTY

(*Pleased*)

Well, good! Now I'm really glad I asked you to stay for dinner.

DAVID

Er—look—aren't you—er—already spoken for by Don?

PATTY

No, of course not. (*She giggles*) Matter of fact, I only met him this afternoon. We met on top of the Empire State Building.

DAVID

(*Grinning*)

Oh. I see.

PATTY

(*Instantly*)

Oh, no, you don't. We may not have been formally introduced—as I'm sure Cynthia was—but I assure you it's every bit as respectable.

DAVID

(*Thoughtfully*)

That is not a reassuring statement.

(*Loud rapping on the door.*)

DON

(*Offstage*)

Hey! It's me! Open the door.

PATTY

Okay—coming!

(PATTY *runs to open the door. Enter* DON. *He is staggering under a huge carton of groceries. His coat and hat are drenched. He starts straight for the kitchen, without noticing* DAVID *at first.*)

DON

Boy—this weighs a ton! I bought enough food for a month's siege.

PATTY

Good for you. Look, Don—we've got a visitor.

DAVID

(*Vaguely*)

Hi, pal!

DON

(*Stares at him*)

What the hell are you doing here?

(*He staggers into the kitchen without waiting for a reply.*)

DAVID

(*Sotto voce*)

Hardly a cordial greeting, you'll have noted. I think I'll fade away.

PATTY

You stay here. (*Calling*) Don! Come here!

(*Re-enter* DON *from kitchen. He looks at* DAVID *truculently.*)

DON

(*Very disagreeable*)

What the hell are you doing here?

PATTY

(*Suavely*)

I invited Mr. Slater to have dinner with us. Don't be so rude. I think you're terrible.

(*The men both stare at her.*)

DON

(*Finally*)

Did he accept?

PATTY

Of course he did.

DON

(*Stiffly*)

Then perhaps I should inform you that Mr. Slater . . .

PATTY

(*Interrupting*)

I know all about it. He's Cynthia's father. But don't worry. He's not a bit sore—and he's not going to horsewhip you.

DON

(*Blankly*)

He's not going to *what!*

DAVID

(*To* PATTY, *reproachfully*)

You talk too much. (*To* DON) The—er—horsewhipping is a—er—feature you haven't heard about yet.

DON

(*Dryly*)

No, but *do* tell.

(*He looks at* DAVID *challengingly.*)

DAVID

Well, you see . . . (*He breaks off and stares at* PATTY. *So does* DON. *There is a moment's silence.* DAVID *smiles at* PATTY) Man talk, honey. Will you excuse us?

PATTY

Okay, I'm going to start dinner, anyway, and you two can gab to your hearts' content. (*To* DON) How do you like your steak?

DON

Very rare.

PATTY

Swell, so do I. (*To* DAVID) How about you? (DAVID *looks to* DON *for a cue.*)

DON

Look, Patty . . .

PATTY

(*Amiably, as to a naughty child*)

Oh, shut up—I'm not talking to you. I invited him, and he's going to stay. You like yours rare too, Mr. Slater?

DAVID

Sure do. Blood rare.

PATTY

Okay. That's all settled. (*Starts for kitchen. Over her shoulder to* DON) If you got your feet wet, go change your socks. They look wet.

DON

Listen, Patty—that stove is quite temperamental. Would you like me to . . . ?

PATTY

You leave it to me. I know all about stoves.

(*Exit* PATTY *into kitchen. The two men look at each other for quite a while.*)

DAVID

That's a remarkable girl.

DON

Yes, she is. Sweet kid. (*Tentatively*) Known her for years. Nice family. (*Removes raincoat and hat.*)

DAVID

(*Poker-faced*)

Lots of nice families live in the Empire State Building.

DON

(*Grins ruefully*)

Oh, my God. I might have guessed. You been here long?

DAVID

Ten—fifteen minutes. She never stopped talking.

DON

I can imagine. (*Shrugging*) Okay—so I picked her up. She's still an awfully sweet kid.

DAVID

Very.

DON

What's the horsewhipping routine?

DAVID

(*Sternly*)

My daughter got in at ten A.M. this morning.

DON

That's right.

DAVID

She was with you all night.

DON

She spent the night in this apartment. That's correct.

DAVID

She claims that . . .

DON

She lies. I never touched her. Moreover, I don't believe you. She'd never say . . .

DAVID

She told me, definitely, that you . . .

DON

She lies.

DAVID

Quit yapping "she lies" in that dramatic fashion before I can even finish a sentence. Let me try to recall exactly what she *did* say.

DON

Go ahead.

DAVID

Well, this morning I was fixing my breakfast—or, to be more accurate, a Bromo Seltzer, when Cynthia came traipsing in wearing a black, strapless formal. You could have knocked me over with a feather. I mean—she's come in late before, two—three o'clock in the morning, but never at ten A.M.

DON

Go on.

DAVID

I asked her where in hell she'd been all night, and she told me she slept down here. No evasion. Just like that.

DON

Yes?

DAVID

So I said to her, "Good God, you shouldn't have done that!" Words to that effect, anyway. I always feel uncomfortable on a high moral plane.

DON

And what did she say?

DAVID

She said, "You're quite right. It was a grave mistake." Then she stomped off to her room, slammed the door and took a shower.

DON

While you searched for a horsewhip?

DAVID

No, that suggestion came later. I stuck around—asked her what she thought I ought to do about it.

DON

And what did she seem to think?

DAVID

She was in a very strange mood. Cynical as all get out. Bitter. Sore as hell. Said she never wants to lay eyes on you again. In effect, that she had trusted you and that you had done her wrong. Her very words.

DON

Even if it were true, I doubt that Cynthia would use such a corny phrase.

DAVID

My theory is that she would use it only if it were true. And she said it several times, "He done me wrong."

DON

Is that all she said? Wasn't she more specific?

DAVID

That's all she said!

DON

(*Slowly, with complete conviction*)

She's lying. I never touched her. Never. Believe it or not. I never touched her.

(DAVID *quite clearly believes him.*)

DAVID

(*Musing*)

You know, it just occurs to me—*that* might very well be the "wrong" you done her. In Cynthia's book. She said—anyway, she was sore as hell. Got me worked up.

DON

(*Coldly*)

Better start working yourself down.

DAVID

(*Burning*)

I can see her point, you know. Don't blame her. Hell hath no fury, and so forth and so forth. I think she's got something. Probably should beat you up anyway.

DON

(*Pacing, frowning*)

Let me get this straight: I'm to be horsewhipped for *not* seducing your daughter?

DAVID

(*Grinning*)

It's quite a new twist, isn't it? However, don't worry. Just an idle figure of speech. Never even whipped a horse in my life.

DON

You're a hell of a father. It's none of my damned business. She's your kid and your responsibility. But does it ever occur to you that your cockeyed philosophy of life may not be what she . . .

(*Enter* PATTY.)

PATTY

Quit picking on him.

DAVID

You see, she thinks I could still be salvaged.

PATTY

(*To* DON)

You did very well, but you forgot the whipping cream.

DON

No, I didn't. Got it here.

(*Goes to get it out of pocket of his raincoat.*)

PATTY

(*To* DAVID)

Why was he bawling you out? I mean—shouldn't you be bawling *him* out?

DAVID

Well, it started off that way—but we got sidetracked. (*Picks up empty martini shaker*) Could you use your girlish charms to promote me another drink? All the martinis seem to have ebbed away.

(DON *gives* PATTY *a container of cream.*)

DON

Here's the cream.

PATTY

Oh, thanks. (*Gives shaker to* DON) He wants another drink.

DON

(*Puts shaker down*)

Want to switch to brandy?

DAVID

I'm not fussy—if you're too lazy.

PATTY

(*On her way out*)

Now don't get him tight, and don't start quarreling again. I like him, he's cute.

(*Exit* PATTY.)

DAVID

You know, that's an exceptionally charming girl.

DON

(*Curtly*)

Yes, she is.

DAVID

Directly after dinner, I'll make myself scarce.

DON

I didn't invite her here to spend the night.

DAVID

It could happen, though. Cynthia spent the night here yesterday.

DON

Do I have to tell you again? She slept in the guest room. I slept in mine. That's how she spent the night.

DAVID

I see. But why?

DON

I'll tell you why. We'd been to dinner and to a show. I brought her home about midnight. Cynthia wanted to come in here for a nightcap, but I said no. We went straight up in the elevator to your apartment. I said good night to her at the front door. Then I came down here. Five minutes later she came back here. She said she'd found you up there, extremely tight, and with—with a young lady.

DAVID

(*Flippantly*)

She was young.

DON

You know, it's really very tragic. Cynthia thought it was rather funny, too.

DAVID

(*Soberly*)

Go on.

DON

You're not going to like this.

DAVID

You think I've liked it so far?

DON

Well, we sat around for a while and had some drinks. She didn't want to go back to your apartment.

DAVID

(*Ironically*)

Too degrading?

DON

No. She said she didn't want "to cramp your style." Said she'd known since she was about eleven that you were helling around with assorted women. . . . Finally she . . . (*He hesitates*) She—well, she . . .

DAVID

Offered to spend the night with you—*not* in the guest room?

DON

(*Quickly, chivalrously*)

Yes, but she was all upset and mixed up. She didn't really mean it.

DAVID

(*Burning up*)

Are you suggesting that she's a moron? She's not a fifteen-year-old high-school kid. A girl doesn't— Of course she meant it.

DON

(*Stiffly*)

I chose to believe otherwise.

DAVID

(*Savage mimicry*)

He chose to believe otherwise. My God, the girl's crazy about you, isn't she?

DON

I don't know—and I don't think she knows. Anyway, now *you* know what the score is.

DAVID

Let me ask you one question—as man to man.

DON

(*Grins*)

When a man puts it that way, it's always bitchy.

DAVID

Okay, but perhaps we'll get nearer the truth. As man to man let me ask you this—and let's forget for a moment that I'm related to Cynthia, shall we?

DON

Shouldn't be hard for you—you're *always* forgetting.

DAVID

Let me ask you this: when a pretty girl offers herself to a man—under conditions such as you've described—what would stop him?

DON

Apart from moral barriers—which we needn't go into—nothing if the man's in love. Then he doesn't mind being committed.

DAVID

Correct me if I'm mistaken, but weren't you sort of engaged to her?

DON

There is an important distinction between an *engagement* and a *commitment.*

DAVID

Aha.

DON

(*Needling*)

As man to man—I was unwilling to lose the initiative—I've given it a lot of thought.

DAVID

(*Growling*)

Intellectual bastard, aren't you?

DON

When you're carrying the ball you don't like to lose it—on a fumble—in a casual bed . . .

DAVID

I'm not a football fan—but is it customary for the ball carrier to function also as the referee? Who blew the whistle?

(*Enter* PATTY *from kitchen, carrying tablecloth. She overhears the last line.*)

PATTY

What are you fighting about now? Football?

DAVID

Why, yes. We were just discussing an incompleted pass.

Curtain

ACT TWO

ACT TWO

Time—couple of hours later. DAVID *is sprawled on the couch sipping brandy from a snifter.* PATTY *is not in the room. She's out in the kitchen washing up.* PATTY'S *dress, looking somewhat limp and damp, is hanging over the back of the chair by the fireplace.* DON'S *mood is surly and disagreeable.* DAVID *is smug and complacent.*

DAVID

Still raining. Yep. Makes for a nice, cozy evening indoors. Put another log on the fire.

DON

'Smatter? You paralyzed?

DAVID

I'm a guest.

DON

And not a very welcome guest, may I add?

DAVID

You made that very clear throughout the meal. I was quite embarrassed. Such a good meal, too. You hardly spoke a word.

DON

Several words occurred to me, but there was a lady present.

DAVID

I did my best to keep the conversation rolling, but I must admit that I detected a slight feeling of strain.

DON

Yes, I thought that some of your jokes were rather strained. However, we'll give you an E for effort.

DAVID

Are you annoyed about something?

DON

(*Grimly*)

Okay, Slater. You crashed the party. You've had your fun. Now why don't you blow?

DAVID

Do you think Patty would like that? I'm here at her invitation—repeated several times—even in your presence. She really twisted my arm.

DON

I feel sure she'll excuse you now.

DAVID

What makes you so sure? I got the impression that she really craved my presence here. She may have had some reason above and beyond the call of hospitality, to urge me to stay.

DON

Your irresistible charm, no doubt.

DAVID

No, I'd say it was a combination of natural curiosity—about me and Cynthia—and feminine fear of spending an evening alone with you.

DON

Don't worry. There was no fear. Before we even came up here I promised . . .

DAVID

My God! You promised . . . ? Then she *was* afraid—afraid of being bored to death. But why should we speculate? Let's ask her why she invited me. I'd be really interested.

(*He rises.*)

DON

(*Accepts the challenge*)

Okay. Ask her.

DAVID

On second thought . . .

(DAVID *sits down.*)

DON

Lost interest?

DAVID

Women are never honest when they're put on a spot.

(DON *laughs and strolls toward the kitchen.* DAVID *sits back.*)

DON

I'm going to help her. Doesn't seem right to let the poor kid do all the work alone.

DAVID

Don't be sentimental. Women love to work. In her case I think it's rather a transparent device.

DON

(*Turning to him*)

What are you talking about?

DAVID

Reached your heart via the stomach . . . The dinner was excellent. Now having established a beach-head in your heart, she's landing in full force on your whole bosom with this dish-washing, see-what-a-superb-housekeeper-I-am routine.

DON

You always look for an ulterior motive, don't you?

DAVID

Yes, and I nearly always find one.

(DON *gives him a dirty look. He shoves open the swinging door into the kitchen.*)

DON

Sure you don't need any help?

PATTY

(*Offstage*)

No, thanks. I'll be through in a few minutes.

DON

Just stack all the stuff. I get daily maid service. You don't have . . .

PATTY

(*Offstage*)

Uh huh. I know. Daily maids are lazy slobs. You just leave me alone and don't stand there kibitzing. Go and read a book or something. . . . What's Mr. Slater doing?

DAVID

(*Calling to* PATTY)

I'm still here.

PATTY

(*Offstage*)

That's good.

(DAVID *gives* DON *a triumphant look as he settles back on sofa, and* DON *goes to get a drink.*)

DAVID

(*Sprawling on the couch*)

Want to play some gin? I took you for a bundle the other night, as I recall. Want to get it back?

DON

Are you planning to settle down for the rest of the evening?

DAVID

(*Raised eyebrows*)

You feel that I'm offering you unfair competition?

DON

(*Savagely*)

I just wish you'd call it a day and get the hell out of here.

DAVID

(*Rising*)

My dear boy, forgive me. . . . Perhaps I'm a little confused.

DON

By what?

DAVID

Well, mainly by you. By your repeated—and quite unnecessary protestations throughout the evening that this was not to be construed as a rendezvous. (*Confidentially*) Now, if you'd been honest and would have come right out and told me . . .

DON

I'd hate to have a mind like yours. Haven't you ever wanted to spend the evening alone with a girl without trying to make her? (DAVID *suddenly sits down*) What's the matter with you?

DAVID

I'm trying to think. . . . I take it you're referring to a young, pretty girl?

DON

You're overplaying it, Slater. You know that's a nice kid. There's a cleaned, scrubbed quality about her that even you could see.

DAVID

The greatest courtesans of history were all cleaned and scrubbed in appearance, as far as I know. Mandatory to the profession, you might almost say.

DON

You know very well what I mean.

DAVID

Okay, but keep the soap commercials out of it.

(*The telephone rings.* DON *goes to answer it.* DAVID *watches him. The kitchen door swings open and* PATTY *enters with plate and dish towel. She wears a man's silk robe over her slip.*)

DON

(*Into phone*)

Hello—no, no—no . . . Yes.

(*He hangs up.* PATTY *stares across at* DAVID *who grins.*)

PATTY

What do you make of that, Watson?

DAVID

Three "no's" and one "yes." Department of utter confusion.

PATTY

I got the impression that he was deliberately noncommittal.

DAVID

Yes, he has a lot of experience in non-committing himself.

(PATTY *giggles.*)

DON

(Prowls around, chewing his lip)

I have to go some place.

(DON *shrugs himself into his raincoat.* DAVID *watches him.*)

DAVID

(Tongue in cheek)

Would you like me to keep her company until you return? I'll be delighted to stay.

(DON *is debating what to do.*)

PATTY

Where are you going?

DON

I have to go out for a few minutes.

PATTY

What for?

DON

It's—er . . .

DAVID

Don't be indiscreet, Patty. When your host walks out on you, never inquire into the reasons. (*Strolls to get his hat and raincoat*) Just finish the dishes, like a good girl.

PATTY

Are you leaving, too?

DAVID

Our young friend has made it clear to me that my presence is undesirable.

PATTY

You mean to me?

DAVID

To him. I think.

PATTY

Well! I certainly don't intend to stay here alone.

(*She rolls down her sleeves, unfastens her improvised apron.*)

DON

Look, Patty.

DAVID

Why don't you take her along with you, Don? Or would that be embarrassing?

DON

I won't be gone more than ten or fifteen minutes.

DAVID

He fears that during that time, I will attempt to alienate your affections.

PATTY

(*Amused*)

Gosh! Sounds exciting. (*To* DON) Don't worry. He's really quite harmless.

DAVID

No comment.

DON

(*Reluctantly*)

Well, okay. But just remember that she hates middle-aged men who make passes.

DAVID

And who can blame her?

DON

(*Crossing to door*)

And you're old enough to be her father.

DAVID

(Flops into a chair)

You're treading on dangerous ground. I'm a hell of a father. Remember?

DON

(At door)

Just leave her alone.

(Exit DON. PATTY *folds her dish towel neatly, walks to kitchen, tosses it onto a shelf.)*

PATTY

(Pensively)

Poor Don. Why do you needle him all the time?

DAVID

Now don't start feeling sorry for him.

*(*PATTY, *at the door, glances around kitchen, then closes door.)*

PATTY

Well, anyway, I really did a job in there. Everything's washed up and cleaned up and put away neat as a pin.

DAVID

Don't be so smug about it. Tidiness is not a virtue.

PATTY

It is so. They always say that cleanliness is next to godliness.

DAVID

Okay. But godliness does not appeal to me.

*(*PATTY *sits down comfortably in a chair and props her feet up on a table, in a relaxed, unladylike position, displaying generous portions of nylon slip and nylon hose.)*

PATTY

What does appeal to you?

DAVID

Steaks—liquor—and sex—in that order.

(PATTY *lowers her legs promptly and gets up. She crosses to the fireplace and casually inspects her dress.*)

PATTY

Oh, you're not nearly as depraved as you'd like people to think.

DAVID

Is it dry yet?

PATTY

I think it's getting dry, sort of. (*She holds the dress up for inspection*) Of course, this stain will never come out completely. There ought to be a law.

DAVID

What about?

PATTY

(*Mock indignation*)

About you. About people who haven't got more sense than to help themselves to ketchup like this.

(*She demonstrates by holding an imaginary ketchup bottle and smacking the bottom of it sharply with a fist.*)

DAVID

(*Grinning*)

Didn't I apologize in the most handsome and servile fashion?

PATTY

You weren't even aiming it at the plate.

DAVID

Oh, stop fussing. You look very charming in that robe of Don's. . . . And you probably know it.

PATTY

That must've been a girl on the phone.

DAVID

No question about it.

PATTY

Do you suppose it was Cynthia?

DAVID

I hope so.

PATTY

I suppose you'd like them to kiss and make up?

DAVID

Sure, I'm all for it.

PATTY

Do you realize we've practically driven him out of his own apartment?

DAVID

(*Piously*)

Let us console ourselves by the hope that we have driven them into each other's arms.

PATTY

What were you fighting about just before dinner?

DAVID

Weren't you listening at the door?

PATTY

No! You can't hear a thing from the kitchen, anyway. What were you . . . ?

DAVID

I was deploring his morality.

PATTY

And you *still* want him to marry your daughter?

DAVID

I deplored his morality, not immorality.

PATTY

(*Relieved*)

Oh. (*Pause*) Wasn't that a good dinner I whipped up?

DAVID

How many times during the meal did I congratulate you?

PATTY

Quite often.

DAVID

You want to get married some day and stay married?

PATTY

Sure.

DAVID

My wife was a Southern girl. Cute little thing. She made popovers, superb popovers. I never ate less than three. I always said "swell popovers" or "wonderful popovers," or frequently, "some popovers." Then, maybe an hour later, while I was still digesting them, she always said, "Weren't those popovers good?" You want to know what happened?

PATTY

You divorced her.

DAVID

No. She divorced me. Extreme cruelty. I hit her with a skillet.

PATTY

You didn't!

DAVID

A stainless-steel skillet. Still warm from popovers. Right across her behind. Raised a welt that lasted for weeks, according to her lawyer. I was never privileged to see it.

PATTY

I don't believe you.

DAVID

Why not? It's the truth.

PATTY

You struck a woman?

DAVID

Certainly. Matter of fact, I rarely strike anyone but a woman. I'm not the belligerent type. I'm also a coward. Oh, once in a while, I'll strike a small, defenseless man.

PATTY

You're making it up.

DAVID

It's a fact.

PATTY

But—but you're a Southerner. They all . . .

DAVID

My child, geography has nothing to do with it. Hookworm, yes; chivalry, no.

PATTY

I think you're simply awful. I'm not surprised your wife divorced you. I'm only surprised that anyone ever married you in the first place.

DAVID

Now don't be silly. A predisposition to knock women about is not a characteristic that a man advertises while he's courting. I *can* be rather ingratiating.

PATTY

Yes, you can. That's your whole trouble. Too much charm. Entirely too much.

DAVID

Would you like to marry me?

PATTY

And be knocked about with skillets? Don't be silly.

DAVID

Yes, it was a mistake to tell you about that at this stage. Grave error. However, you're a strong, healthy, athletic-type girl. Much stronger than my ex. You'd hit back. I'd be more careful. How about it?

PATTY

How about what?

DAVID

(*Soberly*)

Would you like to marry me?

PATTY

Wouldn't you feel foolish if I said yes?

DAVID

No. I would like you to say yes. That's really why I asked you.

PATTY

Do you go around asking strangers to marry you?

DAVID

No. I've asked a few chance acquaintances if they'd like to live in sin with me.

PATTY

Why didn't you ask me?

DAVID

You know, there's a popular theory that nice little girls are always led astray or seduced by nasty old men. It isn't so. For every nice girl seduced by a nasty old man, there are *fifty* betrayed by inexperienced *nice* young men. *Only* nasty old men have an instinctive respect for innocence.

PATTY

You're rather sweet.

DAVID

I might add that since my divorce, I have never proposed marriage to anyone but you.

PATTY

You must be drunk.

DAVID

No. I'm comparatively sober.

PATTY

Well, in that case, you must be crazy.

DAVID

Why? You're on record as wanting to marry a well-heeled man of mature years. I'm forty-one.

PATTY

One wouldn't know it. You act like an adolescent.

DAVID

Should be an irresistible combination. You could mother me.

PATTY

No, thanks.

DAVID

You could mother Cynthia, then.

PATTY

Oh, sure. She'd just love that. I'm all of three years older.

DAVID

She's always urging me to get married to some nice young girl. Well, if Cynthia and Don get together you could be his mother-in-law. Does *that* appeal to you?

PATTY

You shouldn't joke about it. Marriage is much too serious. (*A long pause*) You must be absolutely crazy.

DAVID

For proposing marriage?

PATTY

Yes. What do you know about me?

DAVID

Enough. You're intelligent, you're efficient. You have an adventurous spirit. You're infectiously young and gay. You're an excellent cook. You have a charming face and figure, and you have admirable legs.

PATTY

(*Fascinated*)

Go on.

DAVID

That should be enough for you. It's enough for me.

PATTY

You haven't said a word about love.

DAVID

There are altogether too many words said about love.

PATTY

Nevertheless, a girl likes to hear them.

DAVID

Knowing that nine-tenths of them are empty, pretty lies?

PATTY

They don't have to be, always.

DAVID

I allowed a margin of ten per cent for romantic sentimentalists.

PATTY

I'll wait for somebody in that bracket.

DAVID

Someone like Don, maybe.

PATTY

Maybe.

DAVID

It was my impression that you were looking for a secure, stable, sanctified relationship with a man who would appreciate you.

PATTY

Yes. But a girl wants to be happy, too.

DAVID

I have an immense capacity for making people happy.

PATTY

With skillets?

DAVID

Ended the union with one clean blow. She married a rich Brazilian almost immediately. Happy as a clam, now. Got a handsome settlement, too. Any more questions?

PATTY

I wouldn't marry you if you were the last man on earth.

DAVID

That's an emotional and ill-considered figure of speech.

PATTY

I mean it.

DAVID

My child, if I were the last man on earth—and if there were a million women left, you'd be fighting tooth and claw with all of them for the privilege of being my mate. You'd be panting to repopulate the world.

PATTY

Don't kid yourself.

DAVID

Your loyalty to the human race would overcome your prejudice against me.

PATTY

You're completely wrong. I don't think the human race is so hot. And I'm not prejudiced against you. I think you're perfectly charming. And crazy.

(*The telephone rings.*)

DAVID

Let it ring.

PATTY

You mean not answer it at all?

DAVID

You couldn't bear that, could you?

(*Phone rings again and again.*)

PATTY

It could be an emergency.

DAVID

Somebody wants a house built right this minute.

PATTY

Emergencies can happen to anyone.

DAVID

All right. Don't torture yourself.

(PATTY *picks up phone eagerly. The line is obviously dead. She hangs up.*)

PATTY

Now they've gone. Why didn't you let me answer it in the first place? (*Looks at watch*) What time is it in Europe?

DAVID

(*Baffled*)

Pardon?

PATTY

I was just wondering if it could be his mother. She's in Europe—he told me.

(DAVID *gets up, takes the telephone off the hook, and sits down again. It remains off the hook, unnoticed, for the balance of* ACT TWO)

You shouldn't do that.

DAVID

Why not?

PATTY

Because this is *his* apartment.

DAVID

And we are his guests. He never should have left. No manners.

PATTY

I hope he comes back and kicks you out.

DAVID

It isn't necessary. I'll leave at once if you'd like me to. Is that what you want?

PATTY

Yes.

DAVID

(*Starts to get up*)

All right.

PATTY

(*Smiling*)

But suppose he doesn't come back?

DAVID

(*Settling down again*)

In that case, you'd probably be bored stiff waiting for him. Or, of course, you could always go home.

PATTY

Oh, no, not before I see him. I couldn't. I mean—well, it's been such a crazy sort of evening. I'd have to wait for him.

DAVID

And if he stayed out all night?

PATTY

Where would he stay?

DAVID

There are places.

PATTY

He's not that kind.

DAVID

How do you know?

PATTY

Well, don't you? He *was* going to marry your daughter, you may recall.

DAVID

I asked for no certificate of chastity. Nor, I am sure, did Cynthia.

PATTY

Maybe she phoned from the corner drug store.

DAVID

People often do.

PATTY

Or even from the lobby.

DAVID

Could be.

PATTY

Look, will you promise to leave the instant he comes back?

DAVID

I will promise no such thing.

PATTY

You're a difficult man.

DAVID

However, I'll repeat my offer to leave now, if you'd rather.

PATTY

Where would you go?

DAVID

Upstairs, to my apartment.

PATTY

What would you do?

DAVID

Probably telephone to a dame I know and ask her to come over.

PATTY

Don't say "dame." It's vulgar. At least say "girl."

DAVID

This girl is quite vulgar in the sense that she's earthy and rather uninhibited. By common definition, she is essentially a "dame" rather than a "girl."

PATTY

Isn't that awfully sordid?

DAVID

It isn't spiritual, but it isn't sordid. This—er—character is a lot of fun.

PATTY

(*Ironically*)

Good clean fun?

DAVID

Don't be so contemptuous of healthy carnality.

PATTY

(*Puzzled*)

What's carnality?

DAVID

The sinful lusts of the flesh.

PATTY

Oh! That's from the Bible, isn't it?

DAVID

They've been doing it for a long time.

PATTY

Do you have anything else in common with her?

DAVID

(*Soberly*)

Yes.

PATTY

What?

DAVID

Companionship. Laughter. Friendship—believe it or not. She thinks I'm a very nice guy. I'm extremely fond of her.

PATTY

Why don't you ask her to marry you?

DAVID

Because she's highly intelligent, and would lose all respect for me if I made such an idiotic and obviously unworkable suggestion.

PATTY

(*Long pause*)

Why did you ask me to marry you just now?

DAVID

A: you want to get married. B: it might be a very good thing for me to get married again. C: it seemed to me that you'd make an excellent and stimulating wife. Are you reconsidering? My offer's still open.

PATTY

You know, it's very strange. You're really horrible, and cynical and shallow and selfish and immoral and completely worthless—and I *like* you. I like you very much.

DAVID

Enough to marry me?

PATTY

No, but I could probably do a lot worse. A lot worse.

DAVID

Think it over.

PATTY

Are you rich?

DAVID

Yes. Fairly rich. No, let's face it. I'm rich, period. I've never done a day's work, and if I never do, I'll always have a very large income, even after taxes. Why?

PATTY

I've never even thought of being even fairly rich, but security is a terrific temptation. (*Long pause, and then, suddenly reaching for her purse*) Do you have any idea how much money I've got in my purse?

DAVID

(*Blandly*)

Yes. You have seven dollars and forty-three cents. And a bank book that shows no balance whatsoever. (*She looks at him in amazement*) I'm not psychic. I looked while you were doing the dishes.

PATTY

(*Smiling*)

That wasn't very ethical.

DAVID

I've never claimed to be ethical. Don thought it was rather shabby of me, too.

PATTY

(*Counting her money*)

Next Tuesday, I'm doing a television show—maybe—and I'll get about $62.50. Then I'll have over seventy dollars. Once I had over two hundred dollars. For over a week, I had it. That's one thing you miss, being rich.

DAVID

What?

PATTY

(*Rises, walks around the room*)

The terrific thrill of knowing that you've got over two hundred dollars. It's wonderful. You just feel like going out and spit in somebody's eye.

DAVID

(*Thoughtfully*)

I won six hundred dollars in a gin game the other night.

PATTY

How wonderful! Weren't you thrilled to death?

DAVID

No.

PATTY

Oh, don't be so blasé! You can't be as rich as all that.

DAVID

No, I like to win, naturally. What I meant was this: I was just six hundred bucks ahead—and now I'm asking myself ahead of what? (*He takes out his wallet*) I have it here. Six crisp, new, one-hundred-dollar bills.

PATTY

You're a dope to carry so much money around. I lost a purse once with over twenty dollars in it. I was sick for weeks.

DAVID

(Gently)

Patty, I would like very much to give you the six hundred dollars.

PATTY

You must be crazy!

DAVID

Will you accept it?

PATTY

No. Of course not.

DAVID

There are no strings to it.

PATTY

Why should you give me six hundred dollars?

DAVID

Maybe I'm not as depraved as I think I am—if I may borrow your phrase.

PATTY

No. Seriously. Why?

DAVID

I told you I got no great kick out of winning it. Give me the kick I missed, by accepting it?

PATTY

(Weakening)

But look. I can't take money from . . .

DAVID

I said there were no strings to it.

PATTY

How much is forty into six hundred?

DAVID

(*Pause for mental arithmetic*)

Fifteen. Why?

PATTY

That's what I average. Forty a week. Gosh—fifteen weeks!

DAVID

(*Folds bills, holds them out to her*)

Sold?

PATTY

I don't know what to do. I've never taken money from a man.

DAVID

I won it from a very unpleasant, ruthless capitalist, who grinds the faces of the poor. (*Still proffering money*) Sold?

PATTY

It's an awful temptation. Would you think me a dope if I said no?

DAVID

(*Thoughtfully*)

Yes, but dopes who said no have added quite a bit to human dignity, such as it is.

PATTY

What would your little friend—(*A glance upward*)—the one we were talking about. What would she do? If you offered the money to her?

DAVID

I don't know. I've given her presents now and then. I've never offered to give her any money. I suspect that she'd say, "Thanks, kid, you're a peach," and that she would have the bills tucked in her stocking in two seconds flat. She's a creature of instinct. (*Shrugging*) On the other hand, she might be very indignant. I don't know. There's a vast difference, anyway.

PATTY

You mean because she's your mistress?

DAVID

(*Laughs*)

She's not my mistress, you sweet little idiot.

PATTY

But you said that . . .

DAVID

Having a mistress implies a beautiful, romantic, sentimental, passionate relationship of long standing. This girl would laugh at you if you suggested to her that she was my mistress or anybody else's mistress. In her set, a girl goes with a fella. At the moment, she's going with me. I wouldn't swear to it, but I fancy that she's going *exclusively* with me. Not that it matters. When she elects to go with somebody else, or maybe to remarry—she's divorced—there will be no hard feelings on either side, no scenes, no explanations, no recriminations, no broken vows.

PATTY

You make it sound very attractive.

DAVID

Make what sound attractive?

PATTY

Promiscuity.

DAVID

You don't know what promiscuity means.

PATTY

All right, then—sleeping around.

DAVID

Okay—I'll buy that—and don't let anyone ever tell you *that* isn't attractive—in its very limited way. (*Again proffering bills*) Well, are you going to accept it?

PATTY

(*Moves closer*)

I suppose it would be crazy not to—I mean, it's a fortune. (*Reaches out a hand, and then pulls it back*) Are you a writer, by any chance?

DAVID

Good God, no! Why?

PATTY

I used to know a writer. Last winter, when I had a foul cold, he asked me to go with him to Miami for a week. I was just dying to go, because I needed some sun, but I knew this writer was sort of a wolf. He was in Hollywood once, and he used to date people like Shelley Winters. He said he'd buy me airplane luggage and sport clothes and everything. We had a terrific scene at Lord & Taylor's, because I finally said no. I never saw him again. He wanted to buy me the most adorable lizard-skin purse and shoes.

DAVID

(*Puzzled*)

I don't quite get the point.

PATTY

I'm just coming to the point. Months later, I read a short story of his. It was in the *New Yorker*. It was called "The Jaws of the Alligator." I was furious.

DAVID

Why?

PATTY

Because it was the whole story of our bust-up, that's why. The whole story, word for word. He just changed the names and he made it an alligator purse at Bergdorf-Goodman's instead of lizard skin at Lord & Taylor's. Because of the title, see? He was just using me for copy. I think that was pretty chintzy.

DAVID

(*Poker-faced*)

I vow never to use this incident for copy. In fact, I'll never tell it to a soul.

PATTY

Okay, then. I—I'll take it.

(*She takes the money gingerly. Then, suddenly, she is overcome by shyness. She doesn't know what to say or do.*)

DAVID

(*Kindly*)

Good for you.

PATTY

Gosh, that's the first time I've ever *seen* one! (*Unhappily*) I don't know what to say. I'm completely at a loss for words.

DAVID

(*Smiling*)

Oh, dear. That's bad. It must be unprecedented for you.

PATTY

(*Gravely*)

I know—I do talk a lot. But this . . . (*Shrugging*) Just to say "I thank you" seems so—well, I mean it sounds just silly.

DAVID

Sounded okay to me, the way you said it.

PATTY

It isn't enough, just "thank you." (*Looks at the money*) Fifteen weeks of security, for free. I just don't know what to say.

DAVID

Don't make a production of it, Patty. Skip it. I'm well repaid, already.

PATTY

By what?

DAVID

Your look of wholesome rapture.

PATTY

(*Long pause*)

You know—there are strings—on my side.

DAVID

What sort of strings?

PATTY

Gratitude—affection—a terrific desire to repay you some day—somehow . . .

DAVID

It was a gift—not a loan.

PATTY

That's what I mean by strings. You wipe out a loan when you pay it back. For a gift, you're always beholden. (*She puts the money away in her purse*) Oh, boy, when I show this to Vicki and tell her what happened, she'll fall over in a dead faint!

DAVID

You don't think she'll misunderstand?

PATTY

Six hundred dollars! *Nobody* could misunderstand *that* much. Besides, she knows I don't go in for that sort of thing, and she's a good girl, too. That's why we room together.

DAVID

How about the Princeton man, with the Cadillac?

PATTY

Nothing. It's all very hopeless and sad. They just go to very mushy movies once in a while and hold hands. His wife has very low blood pressure. Or maybe it's very high. Anyway, she's not very healthy.

DAVID

He doesn't sound too robust himself.

PATTY

Oh, you. Unless people are sleeping together, you think there's something wrong with them. (*She looks at him for several moments. Then she leans over and kisses him on the cheek*) There!

DAVID

I didn't like the way you said that.

PATTY

Why?

DAVID

It was patronizing, indulgent and maternal.

PATTY

Well, you offered to let me mother you. Didn't you want me to kiss you?

DAVID

Very much—but without the "there"!

PATTY

(*Amused*)

Oh, you're too fussy.

DAVID

Not at all. The whole point really is—did *you* want to kiss *me?*

PATTY

Of course.

DAVID

You'd have felt pretty silly if I'd said "there"!

PATTY

(*Thoughtfully*)

Maybe you're right. (*Grinning*) Okay, let's try it again. (*She gets up, and after a moment's mental debate kisses him again on the cheek. He is impassive*) That better?

DAVID

Not appreciably.

PATTY

It wasn't patronizing—or maternal.

DAVID

No, but it seemed to be on the daughterly side.

PATTY

Wasn't giving me all that money on the fatherly side?

DAVID

You're too logical. It's unbecoming in the young.

PATTY

Well, anyway, you're sweet.

(*She sits on his knee. Again she kisses his cheek, sweetly and affectionately. He pats her shoulder reassuringly, rather clumsily. Manifestly, this is the first time he ever had a girl sitting on his lap and kissing him without making passes at her. The front door is suddenly opened by* DON, *who comes in very wet, and, when he sees what they are doing, very angry.* PATTY *jumps up off* DAVID'S *lap, startled.*)

DON

Well, I'll be damned! What the . . . ? I'll be damned!

PATTY

(*Fussed*)

Gosh, you did get wet! What were you doing—standing in the rain?

DON

(*Furious*)

Get out of here—both of you.

DAVID

(*Soothingly*)

Now, now, let's not be hasty. (*Philosophical*) Things are not always what they seem to be.

DON

I've got eyes in my head. It was pretty obvious.

DAVID

The obvious is frequently misleading. Now, take little Patty here. She . . .

DON

You take her. You're welcome. (*To* PATTY) You'll have lots of company. He has a whole raft of little playmates. (*Strides to door*) I'd appreciate it very much if you'd both get the hell out of my apartment.

PATTY

(*With spirit*)

Oh, stop being so stuffy and so horrible. Okay, so you found me sitting on his knee and kissing him. Is that so awful? My gosh, I swear I'm never going to kiss a man again as long as I live.

DON

That might be an excellent resolve for you.

PATTY

It never fails. It always messes things up.

DON

And how!

(*He opens the bedroom door.* PATTY *goes to him.*)

PATTY

Don, would you like to know exactly what happened? Why you found me . . .

DON

Does it make any difference, why or how?

PATTY

I think it might. (*Gravely*) You see, Mr. Slater had asked me to marry him.

DON

(*Amazed*)

Marry? He asked you to marry him?

PATTY

Yes. (*To* DAVID, *anxiously*) I hope you don't mind my telling him that?

DAVID

It's none of his damned business.

DON

(*To* DAVID, *still incredulous*)

You asked her to marry you? You only met her a few hours ago.

DAVID

That's correct. One of her dinners and I was putty in her hands.

DON

(*To* PATTY)

What did you put in that steak sauce—marijuana? (*Stepping into bedroom*) I hope you'll be very happy.

DAVID

Wait a minute. She had the good sense to turn me down flat.

DON

(*Skeptically*)

Uh huh. That must have been the close-up I saw when I came in. (*He goes into bedroom, sticks his head out again for a moment*) Again may I say that I'd appreciate it if you'd get the hell out of here.

(*Exit* DON, *slamming the door.*)

DAVID

(*Yelling*)

Which one of us do you mean?

PATTY

Oh, dear, poor Don. What must he think?

DAVID

It's hard to know with such a clean-minded young man. They can think of the vilest things.

(PATTY *crosses to the bedroom door and listens.*)

PATTY

I wonder what he's doing?

DAVID

Maybe he's changing his socks. He looked very damp all over.

PATTY

Look, you'd better go, I think.

DAVID

You mean now—like this—without an honest-to-God scene of some sort?

PATTY

You want him to throw you out?

DAVID

Don't be so melodramatic.

PATTY

He could. He's not a coward. He could easily.

DAVID

(*Considering*)

Yes, but it'd make him feel awfully silly, now. He missed the right moment. Violence should never come as an afterthought.

PATTY

He told us both to get out.

DAVID

Yes, but rather ambiguously. He obviously wants me to blow—but he hopes you'll stick around. He hasn't finished with you, yet.

PATTY

(*Distressed*)

Oh, gosh. (*Staring at bedroom door*) Now he probably doesn't believe a word I've told him. Now he probably thinks I'm just a little tramp.

DAVID

Don't worry about it.

PATTY

But I do. After all, I mean—well, what else could he think? He still doesn't know why I was sitting on your knee and kissing you.

DAVID

And if you have any sense, you won't tell him.

PATTY

He's a very nice boy and I don't want him to think I'm that sort of a girl.

(DAVID *rises, takes his hat, and puts his coat over his arm.*)

DAVID

Are you seriously interested in our young friend?

PATTY

How do you mean?

DAVID

Romantically?

PATTY

How would I know? I've spent practically the whole evening over a hot stove—or talking to you.

DAVID

Physically?

PATTY

Don't be coarse.

DAVID

Matrimonially?

PATTY

I only met him a few hours ago. I'll probably never see him again.

DAVID

But you'd like to?

PATTY

I just don't want him to think I'm a—(*Groping for an appropriate word*)—a pushover.

DAVID

You think he believes that now?

PATTY

(*Glances toward bedroom*)

I wouldn't blame him. He has reason to have suspicions.

(DAVID *puts on his hat at a rakish angle and opens the front door.*)

DAVID

Then take my advice, let them lurk.

PATTY

(*Puzzled*)

What?

DAVID

Suspicions, my child, suspicions. The lurking doubt—is she, or isn't she? Does she—or doesn't she? Will she—or won't she? Suspicion—the most powerful aphrodisiac in the world. (*He goes out, closing the door behind him.* PATTY *starts toward the bedroom. Almost immediately,* DAVID *opens the front door again, watching her*) Now, don't go knocking on the door! Let him lead off.

PATTY

(*Startled, wheeling around*)

You scared me. I thought you'd gone.

DAVID

On second thought, I decided to slam the door. He'll figure one of us is left. Should bring him out panting with curiosity. If things get too unpleasant you know where I live.

(*He waves to her, and then exits, slamming the door as advertised.* PATTY, *very pensive, crosses to inspect her dress, still draped in front of the fireplace. She is disappointed to note that the slam produced no immediate effect. A moment later, enter* DON *whistling from bedroom. He wears a bathrobe, around which he is just tying the belt. His feet are in bedroom slippers. He notes with obvious satisfaction that* PATTY *is alone.* PATTY *looks at him rather nervously.* DON *sits down on the couch and lights a cigarette. There is a long, pregnant silence.*)

DON

Where did Slater go?

PATTY

I don't know. How should I know?

DON

I assumed that by now you would know all about his movements.

PATTY

Well, I don't. And, what's more, I don't care.

DON

(*Very polite*)

Please excuse this robe. I got rather wet.

PATTY

Well, it's a very nice robe. (*Amiably*) Of course it does need mending—where the loop . . .

DON

I have a very gorgeous robe that doesn't need mending. You happen to be wearing it.

PATTY

(*Miffed*)

You shall have it back the moment my dress is dry enough for me to put on. I'd have gone before, but I just wanted to . . .

DON

That's all right. No hurry.

(*He sneezes.*)

PATTY

Gezundheit.

DON

(*Stiffly*)

Thank you. (*He sneezes again and gropes in the pocket of his robe for a handkerchief. There isn't one*) Nuts.

(PATTY *goes to her purse, takes out a folded wad of Kleenex and hands it to him.*)

PATTY

Kleenex.

DON

Thank you.

(*He blows his nose.*)

PATTY

Was that Cynthia on the phone?

DON

Yes.

PATTY

We figured it was.

DON

It was.

PATTY

Have you been standing talking to her in the rain?

DON

Yes. She phoned from Luigi's—that's a cocktail bar at the corner—but I didn't want to go in. (*He sneezes again*) We stood in the rain and talked.

PATTY

What about?

DON

About you, mostly.

PATTY

Me?

DON

Yes. I told her just how we met, and how you came up here to fix dinner—and what a nice kid you seemed to be.

PATTY

She didn't believe that, did she?

DON

She said, "I think I know the type. She sounds like a professional virgin."

PATTY

What an awful thing to say!

DON

Yes. I thought so, too. We had quite a fight about it.

PATTY

(*Gently, musing*)

In the rain.

DON

In the rain. Seemed very appropriate.

PATTY

(*Promptly*)

And? Go on.

DON

(*Slight hesitation*)

That's about all there was to it.

PATTY

Sounds like a very unsatisfactory conversation.

DON

I guess it was. (*Shrugging*) What is there to say to a girl when you—when everything is obviously . . . (*Another shrug, and a smile*) It was raining like hell.

PATTY

(*Gravely*)

I know.

DON

All I wanted was to come back—here—but I didn't expect to find you . . .

PATTY

(*Quickly*)

Necking with Mr. Slater?

DON

Nobody said anything about necking. You were getting along pretty well with him, weren't you?

PATTY

(*Savagely*)

Yes, he's adorable. Too bad you had to barge in just at that tender moment.

(DON *looks at her for a long time. Then he pours himself a drink of brandy and sips it.*)

DON

(*Suddenly*)

I wish the hell Al Smith had stuck to politics.

PATTY

Who?

DON

Al Smith.

PATTY

Who's he?

DON

He built the Empire State Building.

PATTY

Oh. Oh, I see. (*Musing*) Of course, it isn't really his fault. We might have met anywhere.

DON

Do you go around kissing every Tom, Dick and Harry?

PATTY

(*Furious*)

Yes. Yes. Always.

DON

You were kissing him.

PATTY

Yes. Yes. I was.

DON

A perfect stranger.

PATTY

Rubbish. He had dinner with us. I've known him almost as long as I've known you.

DON

I suppose he made love to you?

PATTY

(*Viciously*)

Of course. Violent love. How can you doubt it?

DON

I don't.

PATTY

(*Needling*)

In your apartment, too, to your pickup, wearing your robe and digesting your dinner.

DON

He never had any scruples. I might have warned you.

(*They are working themselves up to a real fight. Suddenly,* PATTY *deflates. She looks at him very earnestly.*)

PATTY

Look, Don. Let's be sensible. Would you like me to tell you exactly what happened after you left?

DON

(*Surly*)

No. What's the difference? (*Unhappily*) It just seems a pity —that's all.

PATTY

What's a pity?

DON

I really thought you were a nice girl. I really did. I told Cynthia you were worth fifty of her. I really thought you were a nice kid.

PATTY

And now you don't.

DON

And now I don't.

PATTY

Mr. Slater does. Still. (*Brief pause*) I think that's why he asked me to marry him. (DON *looks at her contemptuously*) Don't you believe me?

DON

I don't believe he ever asked you to marry him. I didn't believe it when you first told me—or when you asked him to confirm it—or now.

PATTY

Why not?

DON

Because I know David Slater—and he's not the type. That's why.

PATTY

Well, it's true.

DON

Oh, be your age. Slater's a playboy—an avowed rake and a libertine. He's a thoroughly deplorable character.

PATTY

I like him very much.

DON

That's pretty obvious. I gathered that when I came back with the groceries and found that you'd asked him to dinner. If I'd had any sense I'd have kicked you both out then.

PATTY

Why didn't you?

DON

Because I was a sucker. I was willing to give you the benefit of the doubt.

PATTY

Oh, thanks a lot!

DON

You're not even playing it smart. Now if you told me Slater asked you to sleep with him, I could have believed that.

PATTY

We discussed that.

DON

I'll bet you did.

PATTY

I didn't mean . . . Don't you believe anything I told you on the Empire State Building?

DON

No. Nothing. Did you give Slater the same line?

PATTY

It *wasn't* a line.

DON

He'd have laughed in your face.

PATTY

No, he wouldn't. He's much kinder than you.

DON

Kinder?

PATTY

Yes. He found me up here tonight—he knew how we met —and he had every reason to think the worst of me. He didn't. You were gone—how long?—fifteen minutes—and you come back and look at me and talk to me as if I were just a little floozie. I offered to explain what happened. It's really very innocent. You wouldn't listen. Why? Did you think I'd lie to you?

DON

I don't care, that's all. I'm not interested.

PATTY

Mr. Slater believes . . .

DON

(*Pause*)

I believed it too, this afternoon. It's a pretty good act.

PATTY

(*She's almost crying*)

I think you're horrible.

DON

(*Brutally*)

Don't bother to cry. Cynthia tipped me off to that gag. She said that professional virgins . . .

(PATTY *goes to fireplace and grabs her dress.*)

PATTY

I'm going.

DON

Okay. Going up to Slater's?

PATTY

(*Defiantly*)

Yes. Yes—I am.

(*She marches toward bedroom door,* DON *follows her.*)

DON

Unfinished business?

PATTY

Yes.

(*She opens the door. Looks back at* DON. *He strolls away.*)

DON

If you run into Cynthia up there—tell her she won her bet.

(*Exit* PATTY, *slamming the door.* DON *paces up and down savagely. Doorbell rings.* DON *opens the door. Enter* DETECTIVE-SERGEANT MICHAEL O'NEILL. *He is a very large man and also a suspicious and angry man. He is in plain clothes. His coat and hat are drenched. He looks* DON *over quickly, noting the bathrobe.*)

O'NEILL

Your name Donald Gresham?

DON

That's right.

(O'NEILL *strides in, looks around, and heads for kitchen without saying a word.* DON *is at his heels*)

Who are you? What do you want?

(O'NEILL *looks into kitchen, shoves* DON *aside and heads for bedroom. Still completely at sea,* DON *follows. He grabs* O'NEILL *by the arms*)

Where the hell do you think you are?

(O'NEILL *shoves him aside. Opens door to bedroom, peers in.*)

PATTY

(*Offstage, alarmed*)

Wait! I'm not buttoned up yet.

DON

What *is* this?

(O'NEILL *turns on* DON *and hits him in the eye. He falls down, out cold. The door buzzer sounds.* O'NEILL *opens the door and there stands* DAVID.)

DAVID

(*Startled*)

Evening. Mr. Gresham in?

O'NEILL

No, sir. Mr. Gresham is out. . . . (*Glances to prostrate* DON) Out like a light. . . .

(O'NEILL *kneels by* DON'S *side, takes his pulse.* DAVID *strolls over, fascinated.*)

DAVID

(*Casually*)

Did you break his neck?

(DON *starts to stir.*)

O'NEILL

He's coming to. Thirty-five years on the force have taught me just how hard to hit a man.

(PATTY *enters, buttoning her dress.*)

PATTY

Pop! (*Sees the fallen* DON) Oh, Pop, what have you done?

(*She kneels by* DON, *chafing his hands, etc. He's stirring.*)

O'NEILL

Leave him be. Are *you* all right?

PATTY

Of course I'm all right. How on earth did you know I was here? (*Sees* DAVID) Did you . . . ?

DAVID

Me? Heaven forbid.

O'NEILL

'Tis by the grace of God I telephoned your apartment. Your roommate told me where I could find you.

PATTY

Oh, why can't she keep her big mouth shut?

DAVID

Did he find you in each other's arms?

PATTY

I wasn't even in the room. We had a terrific fight—and my father seems to have come barging in and . . .

O'NEILL

Leave him be. You little fool—don't you know better than to come to a man's apartment and . . .

PATTY

Oh, Pop. You don't understand. He wasn't trying to—I know it looks bad, but he—can't you realize that he—he—he's an *architect* . . .

(*As if that explained everything.*)

O'NEILL

I'll hear your story later. Come.

PATTY

(*Protesting to her father*)

Oh, Pop . . .

O'NEILL

Quiet. (PATTY *goes to bar to get a glass of water for* DON. *To* DAVID) Let me ask you something, sir. Wouldn't you have done what I did if you had found *your* daughter in a man's apartment?

DAVID

That's a good question, Mr. O'Neill. A very good question.

O'NEILL

Thank you. Good night, sir. (*To* PATTY) Didn't I tell you about hell fire and damnation? How many times . . . ?

PATTY

Pop, please!

O'NEILL

Come on!

PATTY

(*As she's following her father out*)

Oh, Mr. Slater, do something!

(PATTY *and her father exit. The door is closed.* DAVID *looks at the prostrate* DON, *gets the brandy bottle and glass from coffee table, pours a drink without haste, puts down the bottle and, with glass in hand, steps over the prostrate* DON *near the end of sofa. Looks down at him, slowly drinks, then casually sits on sofa, gazing down thoughtfully at the prostrate* DON.)

Curtain

ACT THREE

ACT THREE

SCENE I

Stage is in darkness. Moonlight streams from windows. The door buzzer sounds several times. After a moment DON *enters from bedroom wearing a robe over pajamas. He snaps on the lights and goes to front door, disclosing* PATTY. *She wears the same suit as in the previous scene.* DON *stands at the door and does not admit her immediately. He is in a very disagreeable state and* PATTY *promptly matches his mood.*

DON

Are you here again? D'you realize it's after two A.M.?

PATTY

Well, I'm very sorry but I couldn't get back before. I came as soon as I could.

(*She tries to step into the room but* DON *is not yet willing to admit her.*)

DON

What do you want?

PATTY

(*Annoyed*)

What do you *think* I want? I want to talk to you.

DON

What about?

PATTY

Well, I certainly can't tell you in two seconds flat—and I can't do it standing out here in the hall.

DON

Why not?

PATTY

All right. I just came back to ask you what Cynthia meant when she said that I was a professional virgin.

DON

(He finally admits her. He closes the door and then follows her into the room)

This is no time to be calling on people.

PATTY

I know. It's taken me nearly three hours to get away from my father! That's why I'm so late. He took me to my apartment and we had the most awful row. He was livid. You should have seen him.

DON

I did. I caught the first show.

PATTY

Well, anyway, he knows now that it was all quite innocent and he said for me to tell you . . .

DON

I'd rather not hear. I've read about police brutality but it never hit me in the eye before.

PATTY

I tried to phone you . . . (*She sees the telephone still off the hook*) Oh, that man. No wonder they said the line was busy. I'd forgotten he did that. (*She puts the receiver back on its cradle and then goes to him. For the first time she gets a real good look at his shiner*) Gosh, that's quite an eye. Does it hurt?

DON

Yes. Very much.

PATTY

(*Judicially*)

My father shouldn't have done that.

DON

(*Grimly*)

Isn't that putting it rather mildly?

PATTY

(*Quite evenly*)

Look, I'm sorry my father slugged you. I said he shouldn't have. He should have asked a few questions first. But he's my father and—well—he's an old-fashioned man. He sees his duty and he does it. (*Another look at his eye*) That does look ghastly. Would you like me to fix it up for you?

DON

(*Very surly*)

No. It's just an old-fashioned shiner—from an old-fashioned father and I'll cherish it as such for several days.

PATTY

It's a horrible-looking eye—but you said a lot of horrible things to me—awful things—so in a sense I think you deserve it richly.

DON

(*Stares at her, amazed*)

Well, I'm filled with remorse!

PATTY

A shiner doesn't last more than a few days. Some of the things you said to me I'll never forget—never. (*She paces nervously*) You should have put some raw steak on it.

DON

(*Irate again*)

If you hadn't invited Slater for dinner there might have been some steak left for me to put on it.

PATTY

Now don't start that again.

DON

(*With indignant yelp*)

Start, my God! Whose fault is all this? Who caused all the trouble? If you hadn't invited Slater . . .

PATTY

(*Very cold and dignified*)

I haven't come back to discuss Mr. Slater. (*A pause, and then, with feminine inconsistency*) Didn't he offer to do anything for your eye?

DON

(*He's off again*)

When I came to, I found your friend Mr. Slater sitting over there like Rodin's *Thinker*—with a snootful—and instead of showing decent sympathy for me, all he did was tell me what a great guy your father was; and when he wasn't ranting about the great moral lesson your father had taught him, he looked at my eye and laughed.

PATTY

Oh, no.

DON

Oh, yes. Finally I got fed up and kicked him out. (*A long look at* PATTY, *still very irate*) Look, it's getting late. What's on your mind?

PATTY

If you'll stop yelling at me, I'll try to tell you. (DON *stares at her fixedly*) And don't glare at me like that. I can't even think when you . . . (*Looks at his eye; quite friendly*) You know, an ice pack would take down that swelling.

DON

(*Grimly*)

And let's not discuss my eye.

PATTY

(*Gravely*)

All right. That seems reasonable enough. Let's discuss . . .

DON

It's late. I'm willing to forego *any* discussion. In fact, I'm willing to write the whole thing off as a hideous nightmare.

PATTY

(*With a long look at him*)

The *whole* thing?

DON

From beginning to end. (*The telephone rings. He goes to answer it*) Hello. Oh, my God, what do you want? Yes. I'm all right. Look, do you realize it's about two A.M.? Oh, no, I left it off the hook. No, Cynthia, no. Let's just forget it. I don't want to talk about it. The fact remains . . .

(*He hangs up slowly, looking at the instrument. As usual,* PATTY *has listened to the conversation avidly.*)

PATTY

What did *she* want?

DON

She's also overcome with concern about my eye.

PATTY

At *this* hour?

DON

May I remind you that you came in person—also at this hour?

PATTY

There's a slight difference. Whose father biffed you in the eye? (*Faintly malicious*) What did she do, hang up on you?

DON

No. Slater just picked up the extension and was bawling her out. He's had a rush of paternal solicitude to the head.

(*He stands looking out of the window.* PATTY *watches him thoughtfully.*)

PATTY

You're tired, aren't you?

DON

I had a hard day.

PATTY

If Cynthia came down now—and cried over you a little—and fussed over your eye—I wonder . . .

DON

(*Turning on her acidly*)

Let's add Cynthia to the list of topics we won't discuss, shall we?

PATTY

(*Very feminine*)

No. She called me a professional virgin. That's what gripes me. That's what I came back to talk about. Not Cynthia—don't worry—only what she said.

(*Friendly but firm.*)

DON

(*Uneasily*)

It was just a rather—unfortunate phrase—and I flung it in your teeth because we were having a fight.

PATTY

Yes, and they were fighting words the way you said them. May I ask you why does Cynthia object to virgins?

DON

Look, nobody in their right mind would seriously object to being called a virgin, even if they weren't one. . . .

PATTY

Okay, but it's this "professional" makes me mad. I'd like to have that explained.

DON

It's not necessary to advertise it. That's really all the phrase means.

PATTY

What's wrong with advertising?

DON

People who advertise are anxious to sell something.

(*This stops* PATTY *cold.*)

PATTY

Oh, oh, I see what you mean. Maybe I yap about it too much. I hadn't met you for ten minutes before I started yapping about how virtuous I was. Then when Mr. Slater came I yapped about it some more, then . . .

DON

Then *quit* yapping!

PATTY

Maybe you're right. One shouldn't put one's cards on the table. That's a silly way to play cards.

DON

(*Uncomfortably*)

I find the topic rather uncomfortable.

PATTY

Why? It's *my* chastity we're discussing—not yours. (*Poker-face*) We could discuss *yours* if you'd rather. . . .

DON

No, thanks.

PATTY

All right. (*Suddenly*) Do you believe in fate?

DON

What kind of fate?

PATTY

Oh, I was just wondering what would have happened if it hadn't rained like crazy and you'd just taken me out to dinner as we'd planned.

DON

I think we'd have had a more conventional date.

PATTY

Yes. We just started off on the wrong foot, I guess. Anyway, I don't think we'd be sitting here now . . . (*The doorbell sounds*) Oh, my goodness!

(*Both are startled. The doorbell sounds again and there is a rapping on the door.*)

DON

Shshsh! (DON *dashes to the bedroom door, beckons to* PATTY *and shoves her in. He closes the bedroom door and starts dubi-*

ously to the front door. Suddenly he notices PATTY's *purse and jacket and hastily puts them in the bedroom. Finally he goes to open the front door. Enter* DAVID. *He wears a robe over his pajamas.* DAVID *comes in uninvited. As previously, he is not entirely sober, yet not entirely drunk*) What are you prowling around for, dressed like that?

DAVID

Never mind my wardrobe. If it shocks the elevator boys, it's just too bad. (*Peering at* DON's *eye*) That's a grisly-looking eye.

DON

So I've observed—with the good one.

(DAVID *promptly goes to the bar and pours himself a drink.* DON *follows him, irritated*)

What do you want? Do you realize it's well after two A.M.?

DAVID

Exactly. That's why I'm here. This is no time for you and Cynthia to be chewing the rag over the telephone. Thought I'd come down right away and tell you.

DON

(*Indignantly*)

I never . . . *She* telephoned *me!* Why the hell don't you talk to *her?*

DAVID

My dear boy—I did. I am hoarse from talking to that girl. Can't get to first base with her. Moreover, I am running out of material. (*Stares at* DON's *eye*) That's the most unpleasant sight I've ever seen.

DON

Get out of here, will you?

(DAVID *pours himself another drink.*)

DAVID

I'm sorry if it's painful, of course—but let's be fair about it. O'Neill had the right idea. Had it coming to you in spades.

DON

Are you still defending the actions of that imbecile flatfoot . . . ?

DAVID

He may be an imbecile, and he may be a flatfoot—but he's a father. He'd have been quite justified in killing you. So would I, for that matter. There is no closed season for seducers. The unwritten law protects us fathers.

DON

(*Contemptuously*)

Unwritten law . . .

DAVID

Look, I'll grant that if somebody would write it down, more people would know just where they stand—but the principle's sound. Man has the right to protect his daughter. Duty to protect her. Now, getting back to Cynthia.

DON

Why don't you *get* back to Cynthia?

DAVID

All right—all right—don't rush me. She's safe at the moment. (*Displays key*) Locked her in her bedroom. Difficult girl, Cynthia. You know something? Spoke to that girl for an hour about hell fire and damnation—Patty's advice, too—never batted an eyelash. Laughed at me. (*Grinning*) Of course I found it hard to keep a straight face. Guess you have to believe in it yourself if you want to put the fear of God in anybody else. Bawled the hell out of that girl.

DON

Isn't this rather belated—this making a noise like a father?

DAVID

You know—that's exactly what Cynthia said. Stopped me cold. Good point. That's why I locked her in her bedroom. Anyway, for your information I have forbidden her to see you or to communicate with you under any and all circumstances. I think.

DON

So I gathered when you cut in on our telephone conversation.

DAVID

Yes, I knew she'd try to call you, but I heard her dialing. Made me quite sore. I'd expressly forbidden her to do that. (*Musing*) Got to do something drastic to save that girl. Flesh of my flesh, after all.

DON

Go to bed. You're breaking my heart.

DAVID

Don't be cynical. (*Goes to bar, pours himself a final drink. Quotes:*) "There is more joy in heaven over one sinner that repenteth."

DON

Okay. Repenteth in your own apartment, will you? I'd like to go to bed. Go away.

DAVID

That's what I plan to do—go away. Go far away. Yes, sir, I've decided to take Cynthia down to Brazil.

DON

(*Hopefully*)

Good idea.

DAVID

Now why couldn't I have had a son? Nobody cares if they lose their virtue. People are all for it. There's no justice.

DON

Go away. Go to bed.

DAVID

Yes, sir, my ex-wife is in Brazil and it's high time she took charge of Cynthia. What the hell do I know about raising daughters? Do Cynthia good to learn Portuguese. Keep her out of mischief. I'll make reservations right now. (*Politely*) Mind if I use your phone?

DON

You've got a phone in your place.

DAVID

I had a phone, but when you called Cynthia up just now— (*He sees that* DON *is about to protest and beats him to it*)— okay, when she called you—I ripped the damn thing right out of the wall. The only way I could figure to keep her incommunicado. (*Well pleased with himself*) Yes, sir, if more fathers ripped more phones out of more walls, more girls wouldn't get into trouble. (*Crosses to phone*) It's only a local call.

DON

All right. Make it snappy.

DAVID

You wouldn't by any chance know the number of Pan American, would you? I had lunch with Howard Hughes once, but didn't get the number.

DON

Howard Hughes is not with Pan American.

DAVID

Don't change the subject. Never mind, I'll get the number from information. (*He puts the receiver to his ear for a moment and is about to dial when he looks at* DON *in a puzzled way*) You got a party line?

DON

No.

(DON *glances around sharply, realizes that* DAVID *must have heard* PATTY *on the extension in the bedroom.* DAVID *listens again for a few moments and hangs up.* DON *comes to him.*)

DAVID

(*Grinning amiably*)

You low-down, no-good, lying, hypocritical son of a . . . I'll be damned. You've got that girl in there now. I recognized her voice.

(*He goes to bedroom door.* DON *tries to head him off, but* DAVID *beats him to it.*)

DON

You don't know what you're talking about. She . . .

DAVID

(*Yelling*)

Patty!

PATTY

(*Offstage*)

Just a sec, I'm on the phone.

(DAVID *looks triumphantly at* DON, *who sits down in a weary, resigned manner.*)

DON

Okay. And wipe that grin off your face. I told her to hide in there. She was just leaving. I didn't know who was at the door. I didn't want her to be embarrassed by . . .

DAVID

(*Holds up a hand to stop the flood of alibis. He is rather ruefully amused*)

You pillar of virtue! Did I tell you how much I hate nobility? I hate hypocrisy more. My God, you really fooled me. I must be slipping. (*Feigning great concern, confidentially*) Of course it's none of my business—since you're not going to be my son-in-law—but doesn't that homicidal father of hers dampen your ardor at all? He'd scare the hell out of me, I can tell you.

(*He strolls toward the vestibule, then turns back.*)

DON

Slater, you're completely wrong. Patty just stopped by for a moment to . . .

DAVID

(*Gently, almost sadly*)

Look, why don't we try to stop kidding each other? It's no skin off my nose what you do—(*A glance toward bedroom*) or even what she does. I'm a little disappointed—maybe even a little disillusioned. But what the hell, she's not my daughter.

DON

Will you listen to me?

DAVID

Don't bother dreaming up alibis. I'm not sitting in moral judgment—either on her or on you. Okay, so she fooled me too. Pity. Seems like such a nice kid. (*Shakes his head*) Fooled me completely. Great pity.

(*He walks toward the vestibule.* DON *looks back in a troubled way toward the bedroom door.*)

DON

Wait a minute, Slater. She'll tell you. (*Calls*) Patty!

DAVID

(*Interrupting*)

No, I'd rather not hear. (DON *turns back to face him. The door of the bedroom opens silently and* PATTY *stands there. Neither of them is aware of her presence*) Just tell her for me that—that I rather hoped she'd wait at least fifteen weeks.

DON

(*Puzzled*)

What?

DAVID

She'll understand.

(PATTY, *who has overheard this, now strides into the room, burning up.*)

PATTY

She certainly will. (*Both men are startled to realize that she has overheard.* PATTY *crosses to* DAVID) How dare you say a thing like that?

DAVID

Well, it wasn't intended for your ears, but I thought it was rather well put.

PATTY

You're just as bad as Don. I think you're horrible.

DAVID

You do?

PATTY

Yes. I didn't think *you'd* have any doubts. What happened to your respect for innocence?

DAVID

You know in spite of all appearances I feel it coming on again.

DON

Look, Slater, why don't you go up to your apartment?

PATTY

You leave him to me. I haven't started telling him what I think of him yet.

(*She opens her purse and starts groping in it.* DAVID *watches her.*)

DAVID

Now calm down. Don't say or do anything that you might regret. (*Handsomely*) I'm beginning to think I may have—jumped to the wrong conclusion.

PATTY

(*Indignantly*)

Just because you happened to find me in a man's bedroom is no reason . . .

DAVID

It's considered good circumstantial evidence.

PATTY

That's a horrible thing to say.

DAVID

In my condition it's almost impossible to say—but I made it.

PATTY

You also said there were no strings—and I thought you meant it.

DAVID

I did.

PATTY

No—you didn't. (*Wisely*) I don't believe it would have entered your mind that there might be anything wrong—if I hadn't taken all that money.

DON

(*Puzzled*)

What? *What* money?

PATTY

(*To* DAVID, *ignoring* DON. *She is still groping in her purse and now produces the money*)

I never should have taken it—and now I want you to take it back.

DON

Will you kindly tell me what the hell you're talking about?

PATTY

I'm not talking to you. I'm talking to Mr. Slater—about the money he gave me.

DON

What on earth did he give you money for?

PATTY

I don't know. Ask him. I don't know.

(DON *stares at* DAVID *in amazement.*)

DON

You gave her money?

(DAVID *pours himself a drink and looks at* PATTY *reproachfully.*)

DAVID

You have a genius for doing the wrong thing at the wrong time. You should be in the State Department.

PATTY

(*To* DON)

That's why I was kissing him. I was thanking him for a gift.

A gift of six hundred dollars. He said he won it playing gin with a bloated capitalist who grinds the faces of the poor.

(DON *sits down with an amused grin on his face.*)

DON

Well, I'll be damned. I'll be damned.

(*He looks at* DAVID *and they both laugh.*)

PATTY

What's so funny?

DON

He won that from *me*. Only last week he took it from me. I'm still bleeding. That was *my* six hundred bucks.

(*Both men are highly amused.* PATTY *is furious.*)

PATTY

(*To* DON)

Okay. Then you take it.

(*She marches over and hands him the folded bills. He pushes her away.*)

DON

Oh, for God's sake. It's his dough.

(PATTY *marches over to* DAVID *and extends the bills to him. They look at each other for a long time. He makes no move.*)

PATTY

I'd like you to take it back, Mr. Slater. Please.

(*He looks at her for another moment and then calmly takes the bills and folds them carefully, still looking straight at* PATTY.)

DAVID

Boy Scouts are supposed to be doing a good deed *every* day. They must have a hell of a time!

(PATTY *isn't quite sure whether he's making fun of her or not. She walks away irritably. For a moment they are all constrained.* DAVID *is still folding the bills*)

I wonder why it is that young men are always cautioned against bad girls. Anyone can handle a bad girl. It's the good girls men should be warned against.

PATTY

You're so right. (*Suddenly*) I'd like a drink.

DAVID

(*Promptly*)

Good idea.

DON

I thought you considered it high school to drink unless you actually craved it.

PATTY

(*Defiantly*)

Well, I crave it now.

(DAVID *goes to the bar and starts to pour a drink.*)

DAVID

Soda or plain water?

PATTY

I'll take it straight.

DAVID

(*As he pours*)

Say when . . .

PATTY

(*The glass is almost full*)

When.

DON

(*Dubiously*)

Isn't that a pretty stiff drink?

PATTY

(*Taking the drink*)

No.

DAVID

(*To* DON)

Haven't we confused this poor little girl enough for one day? Don't *you* start getting fatherly all of a sudden. (*He watches* PATTY *who is sipping her drink very gingerly*) Bottoms up, baby. (PATTY *takes a couple of good swallows.* DAVID *watches her with quiet amusement*) Cigarette?

PATTY

Thanks. I think I will.

(*She lights the cigarette and puffs on it. She doesn't choke but you get the feeling that she might at any moment.*)

DON

You're really going high school with a vengeance, aren't you?

PATTY

Yes. Across the board.

DON

(*Annoyed, sternly*)

Why don't you quit trying to show off?

(*For answer,* PATTY *merely takes another swallow of her drink.*)

DAVID

Now there's a man who's hard to please. Gripes when you're trying to be pure—and gripes when you're trying to be wanton.

DON

(*Gritting his teeth*)

Look, Slater, will you, for God's sake, go up to your own apartment?

DAVID

All right. (*To* PATTY) Want to come with me? I mean if you're seriously planning to embark on a life of sin—I wouldn't attempt to dissuade you.

(DON *shows his irritation and* PATTY *is aware of it and is playing largely for his benefit. She smiles at* DAVID.)

PATTY

You wouldn't?

(DON *goes toward the door of the bedroom.*)

DAVID

We'd be very discreet, of course. Wouldn't want your father to suspect, but I know a very nice little apartment. . . .

PATTY

Gosh, could I have a maid?

DAVID

Sure. And a Cadillac with a gadget.

PATTY

And charge accounts?

DON

(*Contemptuously*)

It's a very bad routine, Patty. I bet you can't act, even on TV. Good night.

(*Exit* DON, *slamming the door.*)

DAVID

There's always roller skating.

PATTY

It wasn't a routine—except the last part. He goes out of his way to hurt me.

DAVID

Young men in love are always cruel.

PATTY

We've done nothing but fight.

DAVID

He suffers too.

PATTY

I'm fed up with being . . .

DAVID

The status to which I presume you're referring needn't be permanent. (*She lets that sink in*) There comes a time, my child, when you should follow your feminine instincts—when understanding is more precious than virtue.

PATTY

I know—but we've only known each other for such a little time. Wouldn't he lose all respect for me if . . .

DAVID

For a gift one is always beholden. Good night, Patty. You're a nice kid.

(*He exits quietly as* PATTY *sits thoughtfully. She is obviously debating whether to take his advice or not. After a few moments she puts down her drink and cigarette, and goes slowly to the bedroom door. She knocks. There is no answer. She is about to knock again when she gets cold feet. She picks up her purse and gloves and runs away, glancing back, fearfully, to the door. For a few seconds, after her exit, the stage is empty.*)

Curtain

ACT THREE

Scene II

The Observation Tower again.

It's about 4:30 P.M. *on the following day. The sun is beginning to sink but it's still broad daylight.* DON *is prowling around minus hat and coat. His hands are plunged in his pockets. His shiner is still quite conspicuous. He goes to the balustrade and stares moodily at the gadget. Almost sheepishly he fishes in his pocket for a dime and drops it in the machine. He looks through the binoculars. His mood is obviously reminiscent. After a brief glance he drapes himself across the gadget and peers out rather mournfully. We should get the impression that for two pins he would call out "Hello out there."*

A moment later PATTY *comes out onto the platform. She wears a different suit, carries a different bag and gloves, but is hatless, as previously. Slowly she crosses to* DON *and leans across the balustrade. They look at each other for a long time.*

DON

(*Finally*)

Why were you in such a tearing hurry?

PATTY

What?

DON

Last night. You knocked on my door.

PATTY

I know. I—I wasn't sure if you'd heard.

DON

I heard. I was shaving.

PATTY

At three o'clock in the morning?

DON

That's right. By the time I wiped off the lather and opened the door—you'd vanished in a cloud of dust.

PATTY

I know.

DON

(*Gently*)

Why did you knock?

(PATTY *considers this for a moment and then comes back with another question by way of answering him.*)

PATTY

Why were you shaving?

(*They glance at each other for a moment and then look away.* DON *starts pacing again.*)

DON

How did you know I was up here?

PATTY

I didn't—for sure. I went to your office. Your secretary said you'd mooched off—without saying a word.

DON

Yes—I couldn't work.

PATTY

She said you were in a filthy temper. (*Amiably*) Why did you tell her you ran into a door?

DON

(*Amused*)

Because I didn't think she'd be interested in the details of my love life.

PATTY

You're crazy. She was fascinated. I told her the whole story.

DON

(*Wonderingly*)

My God, I believe you did.

PATTY

Of course I did. She seems like a very nice girl. Did you know that her husband was a Thirty-Second Degree Mason? I think that's very nice. She . . .

(DON *interrupts her by suddenly grabbing her elbows.*)

DON

Did you get any sleep at all last night?

PATTY

No—not a whole lot. There wasn't much night left anyway.

DON

I didn't sleep a wink and I've eaten nothing all day.

PATTY

You're a dope. Why?

DON

You know damn well why. Because of you. Worrying about you. Wondering what insane . . . (*He holds her at arm's length, still gripping her elbows, and there should be some doubt as to whether he's going to shake her or kiss her*) I nearly went out of my mind when you dashed off—I didn't even know your telephone number.

PATTY

Don't worry—I knew yours.

DON

(*Grinning*)

You don't think it's right for girls to call up men.

PATTY

Well, yes, but—well, I guessed you'd be worrying about me, and I *did* worry about your eye.

DON

Worry is right. What you need is a governess—or a keeper —or a guardian or a . . .

PATTY

Keep going!

DON

Accepting gifts of money from . . .

PATTY

(*Interrupting*)

Say, listen, about that six hundred dollars—can you afford to lose that much? (*She is now thoroughly wifely*) I think that's terrible—gambling for stakes like that. I bet that's a month's salary—or do architects get salaries? Anyway, I'm quite sure you could find far better things to do with your money than . . .

DON

Will you kindly shut up? We're not married yet.

PATTY

Yes, but . . . (*With a sudden smile*) What did you say?

DON

I said, we're not married yet.

PATTY

That's just what it sounded like.

(He pulls her toward him and gives her a long hard kiss. She responds in a thoroughly satisfactory manner. They come out of it smiling at each other. She opens her purse and produces some Kleenex, wiping off his lips.)

DON

Dusty Dawn?

PATTY

Uh huh. They claim it's kiss-proof but they're crazy.

(She crumples up the sheet of Kleenex and is about to throw it off the building but he takes it from her and throws it into the receptacle.)

DON

Want to know what I thought when you smiled at me in the drug store yesterday?

PATTY

I didn't smile till we got up here.

DON

Well, anyway I was thinking of the sun deck on that cabin I'm going to build. I thought to myself that smile would look pretty damn good up there.

PATTY

Did you?

DON

Yes. And then when you lolled on the couch looking at the blueprints—I thought to myself that it would be rather nice to have you along any time I felt like gloating over a building.

PATTY

You mean a lovely boxlike brick warehouse?

DON

And when you were fixing dinner—and even during dinner when you were flirting with Slater—I thought to myself . . .

PATTY

Are you proposing to me?

DON

Well, if I haven't been proposing for the last five minutes, what do you suppose I've been doing? What else can I say?

PATTY

You could say "I love you" in so many words without all this shilly-shallying.

DON

Haven't I said that yet?

PATTY

No, and I want to hear it. I want the real thing—with all the trimmings—an old-fashioned proposal. (*Suddenly*) Do you know how my father proposed to my mother?

DON

Popped her in the eye.

PATTY

(*Laughing*)

Now of course I can't tell you. You wouldn't believe it now. Anyway he wasn't ashamed to come right out and say "I love you." I'll give you that much of a hint.

DON

Okay. Now don't prompt me. (*Taking her face between his

hands) I love you, Patty—I love you very much—even if you are a screwball and even if you are a little bit nuts.

(*They start to kiss again.*)

PATTY

Do they let children up here at half price?

DON

I don't know. Why?

PATTY

Well, I thought it would be rather nice to come up here for our anniversaries—but with five kids, that's going to be expensive.

DON

We can always leave them downstairs.

PATTY

No, I want them to see it. I'm so glad Mr. Smith put up that building. (PATTY *stands on tiptoes and very gently kisses his damaged eye*) There. (*A pause*) Did you mind it when I said "there"?

DON

What?

PATTY

Oh, nothing, never mind.

DON

You're terribly sweet.

PATTY

(*Happily*)

Just think—we only met yesterday.

DON

It happens—once in a blue moon.

PATTY

Once in a blue moon. Imagine charging a dollar-twenty just to ride to the top of an old building. . . .

DON

(*Quickly gives her $1.20*)

Shshsh.

Curtain